CHINA

From Emperors to Communes

by Chris and Janie Filstrup

Dillon Press, Inc.   Minneapolis, Minnesota 55415

To
Kuang-fu Chu
Chinese specialist of the New York Public Library

Library of Congress Cataloging in Publication Data

Filstrup, Chris.
    China, from emperors to communes.

    (Discovering our heritage)
    Bibliography: p. 155.
    Includes index.
    Summary: Presents facts about Chinese history, art, traditions, social life, and recreation. Includes a chapter on Chinese Americans, a glossary, and a map of China.
    1. China—Civilization—Juvenile literature.
    2. Chinese Americans—United States—Juvenile literature.
    [1. China] I. Filstrup, Janie. II. Title. III. Series.
    DS721.F46   1982   951   82-17721
    ISBN 0-87518-227-5

Dillon Press, Inc., 500 South Third Street
Minneapolis, Minnesota 55415

Printed in the United States of America
    4 5 6 7 8 9 10 91 90 89 88 87 86 85 84

Contents

Fast Facts About China

Official Name: People's Republic of China.

Capital: Beijing.

Location: Eastern Asia; China covers more than one-fifth of Asia and borders the North Pacific Ocean and eleven other countries, including Vietnam, India, Russia, and North Korea.

Area: 3,678,470 square miles (9,527,200 square kilometers); it stretches 2,500 miles (4,023 kilometers) from north to south and 3,000 miles (4,828 kilometers) from east to west; China has 4,019 miles (6,468 kilometers) of coastline, including 458 miles (737 kilometers) for Hainan Island.

Elevation: *Highest*—Mount Everest, 29,028 feet (8,848 meters) above sea level; *Lowest*—Turfan Depression, 505 feet (154 meters) below sea level.

Population: *Official 1982 Chinese Census*—1,008,175,228; *Distribution*—80 percent of the people live in rural areas; 20 percent live in or near cities; *Density*—274 persons per square mile (106 persons per square kilometer).

Form of Government: Communist dictatorship.

Important Products: corn, cotton, rice, sorghum, tea, tobacco, wheat; hogs; chemicals, coal, iron, machinery, steel, textiles.

Basic Unit of Money: Yuan.

Major Languages: Chinese; Mongolian; Uigur.

Major Religions: The religious beliefs of many Chinese include elements of Confucianism, Taoism, and Buddhism.

Flag: Red rectangle with a large yellow star and four smaller yellow stars in its upper left corner.

National Anthem: "The East is Red."

Major Holidays: Spring Festival (falls between mid-January and the end of February); Qing Ming (early April); International Worker's Day (May 1); Children's Day (June 1); National Day (October 1).

Photographs are reproduced through the courtesy of Dalton Delan (pages 26, 33, 52, 69, 98, 131), Ann Newman (page 111), Burlington Northern Railroad, the Chinese American Association of Minnesota, Historical Pictures Service, Chicago, Hsinhua News Agency, Alice Ihrig, Lindblad Travel, Inc., and the United Nations, T. Chen, A. Holcombe, Jack Lang, and Shaw McCutcheon, photographers. Cover photo by David Edgerton.

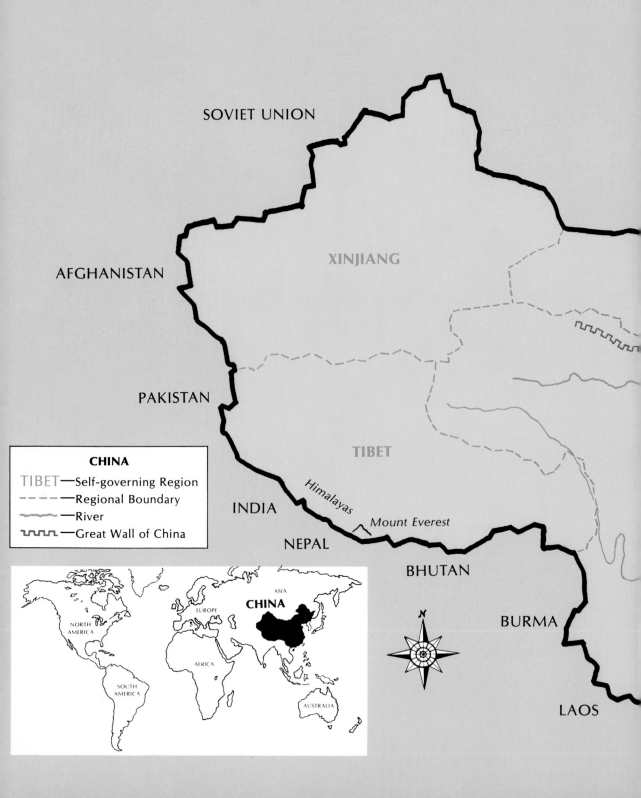

SOVIET UNION

AFGHANISTAN

XINJIANG

PAKISTAN

TIBET

INDIA

Himalayas

Mount Everest

NEPAL

BHUTAN

BURMA

LAOS

CHINA
TIBET—Self-governing Region
---—Regional Boundary
——River
ᴖᴖᴖᴖᴖ—Great Wall of China

ASIA
CHINA
EUROPE
NORTH AMERICA
AFRICA
SOUTH AMERICA
AUSTRALIA

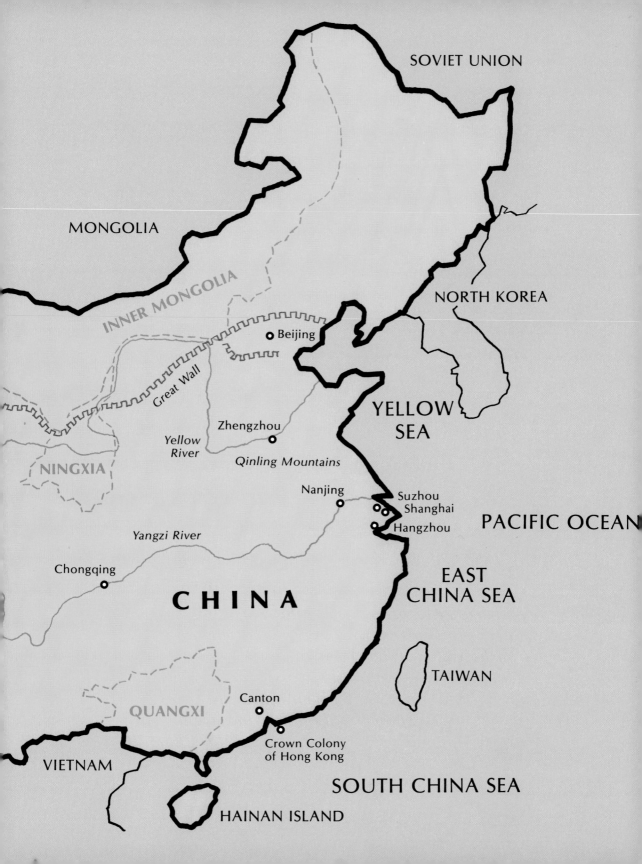

SOVIET UNION

MONGOLIA

INNER MONGOLIA

Great Wall

Beijing

NORTH KOREA

YELLOW
SEA

Zhengzhou

Yellow
River

Qinling Mountains

NINGXIA

Nanjing

Suzhou
Shanghai

PACIFIC OCEAN

Hangzhou

Yangzi River

Chongqing

EAST
CHINA SEA

CHINA

TAIWAN

QUANGXI

Canton

Crown Colony
of Hong Kong

VIETNAM

SOUTH CHINA SEA

HAINAN ISLAND

NOTE:

With a few exceptions, the spelling of Chinese names, places, and words follows the officially approved transliteration system (Hanyu pinyin) *of the People's Republic of China. Old-style spellings of familiar names and places are given in parentheses. For further information about the Pinyin system of writing see Appendix C.*

1. Visitors to China

Long ago, silk, porcelain, oranges, lemons, and fragrant teas—prized goods found in China—passed to the Western lands along the trade routes. Seeing these fine products made many Westerners, especially merchants, want to visit China. They wanted to learn how the Chinese made such beautiful objects, as well as such remarkable inventions as paper, gunpowder, and the compass.

About two thousand years ago, a Roman army

brought back silk from Persia, where it had been carried by camel from China. The Romans were amazed by the soft material, which was so different from their usual woolen cloth. Soon it became popular for both men and women to wear silk gowns, and everyone wondered how such a lovely fabric could be made.

Thousands of years before the Romans, the Chinese had learned how to make silk from cocoons. A silkworm feeds on mulberry leaves for five weeks. Then it spins a little house for itself called a cocoon. At just the right moment, the silk farmer drops the cocoon in boiling water, which unravels it into a long thread of silk. The thread is then woven into a fabric that is light, shiny, and beautiful.

The popularity of silk in Persia and the Roman Empire started the Silk Road. This 3,500-mile (5,600-kilometer) route linked Persia and China. It passed through Central Asia, just north of the mighty Himalayan Mountains. Along this road merchants and their caravans traveled to China to buy tea, spices, and porcelain as well as silk. Profits were high, but the journey was slow and dangerous. It took at least a year to reach China, and bandits or disaster could strike anywhere along the way.

In the late 1200s, Marco Polo, the famous Italian traveler, journeyed to China with his father and

The Chinese learned how to make silk thousands of years ago.
These young women from a commune in Sichuan Province are
gathering the cocoons from which the silk is produced.

uncle. When he left Venice, Marco was seventeen years old. When he arrived in Beijing (Peking) he was twenty years old. The trip had taken more than three years!

Instead of just visiting in China, Marco stayed for seventeen years, working for its ruler, Kublai Khan. The Khan sent Marco to observe what was taking place in China's eastern and southern provinces, as well as in Burma, the Indonesian islands, and Malaya. Marco came from a business family and gave Kublai Khan detailed reports about what he saw.

Marco saw many things in China that Europe lacked. A pony express system delivered royal orders throughout the country. A series of horses could carry a message 300 miles (480 kilometers) in one day. In addition, the Chinese traded in paper money, instead of using heavy coins made of copper, gold, or lead, as Europeans did. They were also mining coal and using it as fuel.

At this time, 100 million people lived in China, while the area that is now America and Canada had a population of only one-half million. Marco told Kublai Khan that 200,000 boats sailed on the Yangzi (Yangtze) River. Hangzhou (Hangchow), a city towards the south, had thousands of public baths and huge covered markets. Entire streets were occupied by doctors, astrologers, and writing teachers.

Other Europeans came to China after Marco Polo. Then in the 1700s, American ships sailed there from Salem and Nantucket, Massachusetts. They sought the wonderful porcelain we call *china*. They also took gold and silver to buy tea, the most popular drink in colonial America. And they bought satin, a soft cloth used as a lining in coats.

The British wanted Chinese goods, too. Every prosperous family had to have its tea and china. To pay for them, the English took opium, a drug that grew in India, to China. At first the Chinese used small amounts of it as a medicine for arthritis and dysentery. Later the British tried to expand their trade by encouraging the Chinese to use the drug as a means of escaping from problems and worries.

So many people started taking opium that the emperor banned all trade with the British. But these nineteenth-century visitors to China were more than just merchants. They were empire-builders, determined to rule the world. In 1840 the British sailed their great warships into the harbor of Canton and bombarded the port. The Chinese had no arms or ships to match the British frigates. As a result, the emperor was forced to agree to let the British bring in more opium. The British merchants had gotten their way, but the Chinese never forgot what had happened.

From 1840 to 1945, the most important visitors to China were from nations that wanted to build an empire. The British, French, and Japanese all came to conquer China. When Mao Zedong (Mao Tse-tung), the Communist leader, and his army took over China in 1949, they wanted it to be left alone. The United States government and other Western powers opposed Mao, so he barred most Americans and Europeans from trading or traveling in China. Westerners said he had put up a Bamboo Curtain.

From 1949 to 1972, not many Europeans or North Americans visited China. One of the few who did was a reporter from the United States named Edgar Snow. In 1936 Mr. Snow was working in Beijing. His job was to send reports about China to newspapers in England and the United States.

At the time, the Nationalist government, led by Chiang Kai-shek, was fighting the Communists, led by Mao Zedong. The Nationalists had come to power in 1928 by defeating the military leaders who had been in control of China since 1916. Beginning in 1934, the Communists had fled from the Nationalist army by marching 6,000 miles (9,600 kilometers) from Jiangxi province in the south to Shaanxi province in the north. Chiang called Mao and his followers "Red Bandits." But Edgar Snow decided to see for himself what they were like.

He persuaded Chiang's army to let him travel to the northern battlegrounds. There the Nationalists were face-to-face with the Communists. One night, Snow hired a mule driver to take him to the enemy side. At Yan'an Snow introduced himself to Zhou Enlai (Chou En-lai), Mao's right-hand man. Zhou was delighted to see an American and took him on a long tour of the Communist-held province.

What did Snow find? Not "Red Bandits," but government officials who were honest. He also discovered that children in the province went to school free. In addition, farmers did not have to give half their crops to landlords anymore—there were no landlords! The farmers worked together to sow seeds and harvest crops.

Later Snow met Mao, who was living in a cave. The walls of the cave were covered with maps and the floor with books. Mao loved to read and to write poetry. He wrote several poems for his new American friend.

Snow was impressed with Mao and the hard-working society he was guiding. In the rest of China, people had to bribe government officials to get their help, and wealthy landlords let peasants starve. Educated people knew poetry, but they never had to work with their hands.

These sharp divisions in Chinese society had been

weakening the country for a long time. During the 1930s and 1940s more and more people, especially the peasants, looked for a leader who could bring the nation together and give them a better life. Edgar Snow believed that they had found that leader in Mao Zedong.

The articles and books Snow wrote after meeting Mao gave Americans first-hand knowledge of the Communists. After Mao took over, he let Snow come to China as often as he wished. Snow was the West's best link with China as it changed itself into a socialist society.

Then, in 1972, Mao Zedong invited President Nixon of the United States for a week's visit. This invitation broke the ice that had formed during twenty-five years of hard feelings between the two nations. The whole world watched while the American president met with Mao. Nixon also toured the Great Wall and visited Hangzhou, a city Marco Polo had enjoyed nearly seven hundred years earlier.

Since Nixon's trip, many Westerners have traveled to China. Among the visitors are Chinese Americans who once lived there. When Mao took over the country, many families were split. Part of the family went to live on the island of Taiwan, while the rest stayed on the mainland. Kuang-fu Chu, for example, was a pilot in the Nationalist air force when

In 1949 Kuang-fu Chu left China for Taiwan at Chien Ch'iao Airport. Thirty years later he returned to China from the United States, landing at the very same airport!

Chiang Kai-shek retreated to Taiwan. Mr. Chu ended up in Taiwan, while two of his brothers stayed in China. They were farmers in Ma-da-shi, a small village 200 miles (320 kilometers) from Shanghai.

Mr. Chu later came to the United States and worked in the news business and as a librarian. From 1949 until 1978, he had no letters from his brothers. Nor could he write to them. But six years after Nixon's visit, when icy relations between the two countries had thawed, he was able to send letters. Soon afterwards he planned a trip home. And in 1979, thirty years after leaving China, Mr. Chu returned to Ma-da-shi.

During his thirty years away, his village had grown from 100 households to 150. His brothers still lived in the house where Mr. Chu grew up, and they still worked the rice fields. Now, though, instead of owning small plots, they labored as part of a commune. The house still belonged to the brothers, but the land belonged to everybody.

When Mr. Chu was a child, most of the village did not have enough food. During the last two months before harvesting the rice, four out of every five people ran out of supplies and had little to eat. Today there is plenty of rice for all.

After Mr. Chu had gone to Taiwan as a pilot in 1949, a rumor began that he was commander-in-chief of the Nationalist air force. The rumor was false, but because Mr. Chu could not write to his brothers, people believed it. As a result, life was difficult for his brothers. Communist Party officials in the area were suspicious of them and blamed them for having a close relative who held such a high position in Taiwan. Imagine everybody's surprise when Mr. Chu's letter arrived from America, saying he was a librarian!

When Mr. Chu arrived in Ma-da-shi, he was welcomed as an honored guest. Communist Party officials wanted to learn all about America. They asked Mr. Chu to give a speech on how America had become so modern. The children wanted to hear about American basketball. And so Mr. Chu went to his old school and described how tall American professional basketball players were and how well they played. During his one-week stay, Mr. Chu received visitors from early morning until late at night in the small house where he had lived as a child.

Then Mr. Chu traveled to Shanghai. When he was a boy, Shanghai was a fun city. Sailors and merchants from all over the world came to Shanghai to buy, sell, and have a good time. Thirty years later, the nightclubs, gambling houses, and fancy stores did not exist. The foreigners had vanished. The Shanghai Club, which had boasted about having the longest bar in the world, was now a seaman's restaurant. The country club had become a government school. A library and a public park occupied the land once used for a racecourse. And the big department stores on Nanjing (Nanking) Road were owned by the government and sold simple goods that everyone could afford.

Other Americans who visit China these days are going for the first time. The places they most like to see are Hangzhou, the Great Wall, and Beijing. Hangzhou is a beautiful city southwest of Shanghai that lies on a bay. Its famous West Lake Park contains many gardens, statues, and temples.

Hangzhou is not only a beautiful city that attracts many tourists, but a busy port as well.

One of the most famous attractions in all of China is the Great Wall. It is the largest structure in the world. If one end of the wall was placed in New York City, and the wall was stretched straight across the United States, the other end would sit in the Pacific Ocean. When the astronauts and cosmonauts orbit around the earth, the Great Wall is the only human-made object they can see.

Visitors to Beijing usually go to Tian An Men Square, at the entrance of the Imperial City. Tian An Men means the "Gate of Heavenly Peace." In the old days this gate divided the commoners from the rulers. But since October 1, 1949, it has been open to everyone. For on that date Mao Zedong announced here that the Communists had defeated the Nationalists, and that the square belonged to the people.

To celebrate the tenth anniversary of this victory, the Chinese enlarged the square. It is now the largest city square in the world, with an area of almost eighty-five acres (thirty-four hectares). One million people can gather here to listen to Chinese leaders. On the west side stands the Great Hall of the People. It has a banquet hall that regularly has dinner programs for 5,000 people and an auditorium that seats 10,000.

How can all these people hear the speakers in the auditorium? In the back of every seat is a tiny loudspeaker. Alone each loudspeaker produces only a faint whisper. But together the 10,000 loudspeakers fill the hall with a voice or music. This is the Chinese way—joining together individual efforts to produce great things.

Tian An Men Square lies at the southern edge of the Imperial City. This area includes lakes and parks built by the emperors. Today it contains some government offices, but the rest is a public park.

Tian An Men Square lies at the entrance to Beijing's famous Imperial City. The square is so large that a million people can gather in it to hear speeches or celebrate national holidays!

The Imperial City surrounds the Forbidden City, which includes palaces of former emperors. Once only members of the emperor's household could enter the Forbidden City. Now it, too, is open to the public.

Tourists are not the only visitors in China today. Students go to learn Chinese. Manufacturers of porcelain go to study old vases and dishes. Business people go to sell grain, petrochemicals, and tractors, or to buy cotton, textiles, peanuts, and crude oil.

As China opens its doors to outsiders, more and more people will travel there. Few of them will stay as long as Marco Polo did, but all of them will find it as fascinating as he did. For there is much to enjoy and much to learn from in this great country.

2. China Today

We drink Chinese tea and eat Chinese food. Our dishes are often called china, and we know and do business with Chinese people. But their culture—the way they think, feel, act, and live—is far different from our own. Indeed, Chinese culture is like no other culture.

The following notes from the diary of a recent traveler to China show what makes it such a different country:

Bicycles . . . bicycles . . . bicycles . . . 200 million of them (one out of [every five Chinese] owns one).

Plain clothes . . . no jewelry . . . only stainless steel wristwatches.

Courtesy . . . reasonable happiness . . . discipline; a relaxed people.

Cities without pet cats, dogs, birds ([keeping them is] against the law).

Very few fat men and women; rarely any fat children.

Equality—in dress, service, work, salary.

Respect and affection for old people (who live with the family—no retirement homes in China).

Stifling dust and air pollution in the larger cities.

Hardly any flies or insects, except in the communes where cattle, horses, and chickens are raised . . . and even there they are scarce.*

These details from the traveler's dairy point to several distinct features of the Chinese culture. First,

*Note: These observations came from Dr. Jay Arena, former president of the American Academy of Pediatrics. They are adapted from the extracts of his trip-book that appeared in the academy's newsletter.

as the millions of bicycles suggest, there are a great
many people in China—over one billion! Because of
this huge population, the people must work hard to
produce enough food and manufactured goods to
meet their basic needs. Indeed, everyone is expected
to contribute to this effort.

Yet it is very hard to provide for so many people
without limiting the amount of money or possessions
one person can have. And so the Chinese believe that
everyone should live in much the same way. They
dress alike, have similar homes, and earn nearly equal

*As this crowd of happy looking youngsters shows, China has
an enormous population—over one billion, or nearly one-
fourth of the earth's people!*

Dalton Delan

wages. Some of them may prefer to live differently, but on the whole they are a happy people who value simple customs, politeness, and family life.

The Chinese live in a land that is as interesting as their culture. It has huge plains and vast deserts, high mountains, and many lakes and rivers. One of its rivers, the Yangzi, is the third longest in the world. Beginning high in central China near the border with Tibet, the Yangzi flows east across the country and empties into the East China Sea.

Slightly south of the place where the Yangzi

China has a great many long and winding rivers. Some of them can still be crossed by narrow but sturdy footbridges.

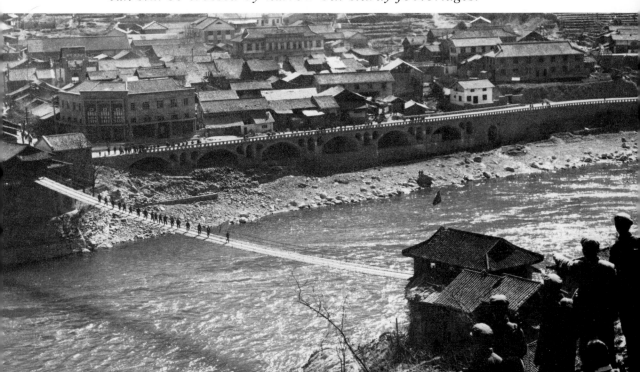

meets the sea is Shanghai, China's largest port. Large ships can enter the river here and travel 700 miles (1,120 kilometers) upstream. Junks and steamboats can go 1,000 miles (1,600 kilometers) farther, past Chongqing in Sichuan Province.

Shanghai was once called the Wonderland of the Adventurers because it attracted so many foreign traders. English, French, German, and Japanese-speaking merchants did business in the city. Many of the old Western-looking hotels in which they stayed and the warehouses in which they stored their goods are still standing.

Today Shanghai ranks as the largest city in the world. Still a busy port, it is China's biggest industrial center. Over eleven million people live in the city, many of them in sections once occupied by foreigners.

Nine million people live in Beijing, China's second most populated city. The capital of the country, it is located in northeastern China and is spread over 6,873 square miles (17,870 square kilometers) of land.

Beijing is both the oldest and the newest city in China. Many of its buildings, such as the golden-roofed, one-story tiled palaces of the emperors, are hundreds of years old. Beijing also has many new government buildings and a subway that runs straight through the city.

Dry plains lie to the north and the west of Beijing. Strong winds often blow the dirt from these plains into the city, making it a very dusty place. Beijing's air is also polluted by the coal that the Chinese use to heat their homes. Every province in China has coal mines, making it the world's largest coal producer.

Recently, Beijing has had a facelift. Hundreds of thousands of trees and shrubs, and millions of square yards of grass were planted. They not only make Beijing more beautiful, but they help to fight winter dust storms by blocking the winds that blow in from the dry plains.

South of Beijing is the ancient city of Nanjing (Nanking). Lying on the south bank of the Yangzi River, it is surrounded by the Purple Mountains. Two and a half million people live in this city, which has been China's capital several times in the past.

The Nanjing Bridge that spans the Yangzi connects northern and southern China. Some 400 miles (640 kilometers) north of this bridge over the Yangzi is another great river, the Huang Ho, or Yellow River. It is separated from the Yangzi by the Qinling Mountains, a 1,000-mile (1,600-kilometer) range that forms a natural dividing line between north and south.

Winding 2,500 miles (4,000 kilometers) through China, the Yellow River frequently causes terrible floods. Sometimes it changes its course, destroying farms and human life. For these reasons, it is sometimes called China's Sorrow.

The river is named for the fertile yellow soil it picks up along its course and carries to the Yellow Sea. This fluffy soil, called loess, is blown into the air during times of drought and later settles into the water. It gives both the river and the sea their yellow color.

Part of the Yellow River flows through central China, the country's heartland. Located south and west of Beijing, it has beautiful river valleys, towering mountains, and deep gorges. These features are often seen in traditional landscape paintings.

Summers in central China are intensely hot, the winters are cold, and the growing season is long. Wheat, corn, cotton, and sorghum are the region's chief crops. In the Sichuan Basin most crops are grown on terraced fields, level strips of land cut out of the hillsides.

Most of the people who live in central China are members of the country's largest ethnic, or national, group, the Han people. The Han speak Northern Chinese, or Mandarin, which is China's official language. People in other parts of China also read and write this language, but they speak it differently.

To the northeast of central China is Manchuria, a

Towering mountains and deep gorges are found in central China, the country's heartland.

region known for its rich natural resources, especially timber, iron, and coal. To the north of the heartland is Inner Mongolia, a vast area of rugged mountains and deserts, including the Gobi Desert. Farther northwest is Xinjiang (Sinkiang), which is much like Inner Mongolia. And to the west of central China is Tibet, a cold and very dry territory, consisting of a plateau surrounded by very high mountains.

Inner Mongolia, Xinjiang, and Tibet, along with Quangxi and Ningsia, are autonomous, or self-governing regions, which have large numbers of non-Chinese people. At first the Communists ruled these people harshly, allowing them little independence. Now the local governments in each region have been given some power to protect the ways and interests of the non-Chinese groups.

China's mountainous regions are home to many different animals. In the high, cool regions, bighorn sheep and big elks called wapitis can be found. Tall, strong deer named samburs and little musk deer also roam through the mountains. Another mountain animal is the Asiatic black bear. Many Chinese believe that the meat and bones of these bears have special healing powers. And they are especially fond of the giant pandas, which eat bamboo shoots and live on upper mountain slopes in southwestern China.

The southern and southwestern areas of China are hot and humid—almost tropical. Tigers, leopards, monkeys, and wild boars wander through the jungle-covered hills of the far south. Farmers in these areas use the long-horned buffalo to help them do their work because it can trudge through their muddy fields. Many farm families raise pigs, chickens, and ducks.

The Chinese do not eat much meat or poultry,

Dalton Delan

High in the mountains of Sichuan Province, a young villager and her daughter make their way along a well-traveled path.

however. Pork is their favorite meat, but it must be rationed so that everyone can have a share. Grains and vegetables are much more plentiful, and they are the main foods in the Chinese diet. This diet includes no milk products. Since it is very low in fats, it helps both adults and children to stay slim.

A great deal of rice is grown in southern China, which is mainly a rural area. The only major city in the south is Canton, a large industrial and trading center that lies along the Pearl River. Canton links this region to the sea and to the British colony of Hong Kong.

Many of the products China exports—sugar, fruits, tea, silk, timber—are loaded on ocean-going ships in Canton's port. In addition, twice a year the city holds a large trade fair that attracts thousands of foreign merchants. Much of the industrial equipment that China buys is imported into the country through Canton.

Few automobiles are brought into China, though, because most Chinese cannot afford to own or operate them. In fact, all of the automobiles in the country are publicly owned. But millions of people have bicycles. Everywhere in China they are the most popular means of transportation.

Beijing has the most bicycles of any city in the world—about three million. People ride them to

Rice paddies like this one can be found throughout southern China. More rice is produced in China than in any other country.

work, use them for shopping, and take short trips on them. Bicycles are even more important in the countryside, even though people must often travel over rough or steep roads. Commune workers use them to reach distant fields. Parents take their children on bicycles to visit relatives or to shop in town. And bicycles are used to carry everything from wood timbers and bales of cotton to live pigs.

Forty percent of the bicycles manufactured each year are assigned to country folk, but this supply still falls short of the demand for them. Nevertheless, Chinese officials view the increase in the number of bicycles as a key sign that working people have a better life than they once did.

These officials are also proud of the steps that have been taken to improve public health. When the Communists came to power, they began a campaign to make China cleaner. They taught people how to dispose of waste products in a proper manner. They also worked to control disease-carrying flies and mosquitoes as well as other insects. Both these measures have made the country a healthier place in which to live.

Food supplies have also increased since the Communists began to govern China. When they took over the country, there was not enough food for everyone. But they were able to improve this situation by establishing a collective system of farming. Under this system crops are raised by groups of people rather than individuals, and more land is brought into use. It has enabled Chinese farmers to provide almost all of the food people need.

To make sure that everyone would have enough to eat, the Communists outlawed all pets. They believed that food needed for human beings should not be given to dogs or cats. They also thought that pets were a luxury. In their view only animals that could be raised for food or used for work were necessary to life.

The Communists also greatly control people's lives. For example, college students in Zhengzhou, capital of Henan Province, on the vast North China Plain, must follow a rigid schedule. Every day at 5:30 A.M. they are awakened by blaring military music broadcast from loudspeakers. After dressing, they have an army-style exercise period which is led by a gruff-voiced teacher. At 7:00 A.M. breakfast—rice and hot water—is served.

Morning classes run until noon, with another exercise session shortly after ten o'clock. At lunch students are served a second meal of rice, although vegetables are poured over it this time. After eating, the students can rest until 2:00 P.M., when loudspeakers again broadcast noisy but dull band music. This music is to remind everyone that afternoon classes begin in thirty minutes.

Free time begins at 4:30 P.M., with yet another exercise period. Around 5:30 P.M., music, announcements, news, and political messages are played over the loudspeakers. Dinner is at six o'clock. However, students must wait in a long line to get their evening meal—rice topped with vegetable or meat sauce. They usually eat this meal in their own small rooms, which have only a few pieces of furniture and concrete walls, floors, and ceilings.

After dinner, students do schoolwork or watch television in one of their classrooms. Not many entertaining shows are broadcast, though. Typical programs include "A Tour of Shanghai General Petrochemical Works," "How to Make a Woman's Dress," and "Health and Hygiene." As you might expect, most students find these programs rather dull, and they are usually back in their rooms and asleep by ten o'clock.

Working people also have little control over their lives under the Communists' system. The government chooses their jobs for them and assigns them to a work unit. Teachers at a college, electricians in a factory, and nurses in a hospital all belong to work units.

These work units make choices about things that most Westerners decide for themselves. The units assign apartments, set salaries, and distribute ration coupons for grain, cotton, cooking oil, and coal. In addition, they determine who can buy TV sets, bicycles, and sewing machines. Work units can even tell married couples when they can have the one baby that the government now permits!

Communist views and policies continue to hold sway in China. For as the diary entries quoted at the beginning of this chapter indicate, the Chinese work hard and live simply. They do not spend their money on fashions, jewelry, automobiles, pets, or costly entertainment. They wear what is practical, travel on bicycles, and enjoy inexpensive sports, movies, plays, or other activities.

The diary also noted that the Chinese are courteous in public and very respectful of old people. These are old Chinese values. As we will see in the next two chapters, China has an ancient culture and history. The new grows out of the old. In many ways, modern China is the China of the past.

3. Speaking Through the Arts

Talking and writing are two of the most important things that human beings do. Without language, people could not think about the past, or plan for the future. Without language, there would be no government, no stories, no jokes, no religion.

Which language a country speaks determines how its people think. It determines how they share information with one another. Yet to the Chinese language and writing are more than useful tools.

They think of themselves as Chinese because they speak and write the Chinese language.

Language is important to all their arts. In opera, the favorite type of music in China, words are sung. Chinese artists express their feelings by writing a phrase on a painting or just by signing their names. Other Chinese write by using a brush on bamboo or silk, scissors on paper, or a sharp tool on wood. In many ways, musicians and singers, painters and craftspeople are forever dressing language up!

English and Chinese are very different languages. In English, we have present, past, and future tenses. The Chinese don't have any. *Ta kan jian yue liang* can mean, "He sees the moon," "He saw the moon," or "He will see the moon." A speaker or writer will use an adverb such as *yesterday* or *soon* to indicate past or future time. What time is meant can also be understood from the sentences that come before this one.

In Chinese, nouns have no singular or plural. *Fangzi* means "house" or "houses." You say *i jian fangzi* to mean "one house" and *hen to fangzi* to mean "many houses." But the word for house—*fangzi*—stays the same.

In English, we call our brothers and sisters by their first names. In Chinese, the children in a family are known as "first brother" or "youngest sister."

What their families call them depends on the order in which they were born. And children avoid referring to their mothers or fathers by the pronoun *you*. That would be very impolite. Instead, the Chinese use a title of respect when they speak to a parent.

The Chinese are very conscious of a person's age and rank when they talk to someone. For example, Kuang-fu Chu, the Chinese American we met in chapter one, has an assistant named Amy Lam. At work she calls him *Chu Po-po*, meaning "Uncle Chu." He is not really her uncle, but in Chinese *po-po* ("uncle") shows respect. In fact, the title po-po shows greater respect than the Chinese word for *sir*.

If you heard Amy and Mr. Chu talk, you might think they were speaking loudly. Indeed, people sometimes think that Chinese speakers are shouting at each other. But the Chinese are not hard of hearing or being rude. Rather, they are making themselves understood by emphasizing a word's pitch, or sound.

If a Chinese says *ma* keeping her voice at an even pitch (∼∼∼∼), she means "mother." However, if she lets her voice drop (⌒＼＿), she means "scold." If she makes her voice rise (＿＿／), she means "hemp," the fiber used to make rope. And if she lets her pitch dip and then rise (＼＿／), she means "horse."

In English, "mom" means "mother" no matter

how it is pronounced. But how the Chinese say a word can completely change its meaning. And so they speak loudly to make the pitch clear.

The Chinese also write their language in a special way, using strokes instead of letters. In English, letters such as *a*, *b*, and *c* represent sounds, and they combine to make words. Strokes, however, combine to make characters, which usually stand for a thing or an idea, not a sound. Picture characters look like the objects they represent. Other characters, called ideographs, suggest an idea rather than an object.

Nine picture characters and their meanings are shown on the next two pages. The first four characters—for mouth, door, mountain, and paddy-field—are meant to show what these things look like.

—mouth   —door   —mountain   —paddy-field

The character for the sun used to be round like the sun itself. Over the centuries, the character was squared off in order to make it easier to write.

—sun   —moon

"Moon," which used to be crescent-shaped, was also squared off for the same reason. The next set of symbols shows how picture characters can be combined. The first character stands for "tree." The second combines the tree-shaped characters to mean "clump of trees." And the third combines three tree characters to mean "forest."

—tree   —trees or bush   —forest

The characters shown on page 45 are examples of words that are related to each other. The first character means "water." It is combined with other characters to express things or ideas having to do with water—river, ocean, clean, clear, and so on. The characters are pronounced differently, however.

—*shui* ("water")

—*hsi* ("clean"; "wash")

—*po* ("wave")

—*chiang* ("river")

—*ch'ing* ("clear")

—*hu* ("lake")

—*yang* ("ocean")

—*lei* ("tears")

Chinese children learn many words automatically. But they must memorize how each word is written. Knowing the sound of a word does not help them write it.

Written Chinese has about 50,000 characters, or words. To read a newspaper a Chinese must know around 5,000 characters. To read important works of

Chinese literature such as the *Sayings of Confucius*, a guide for government written by the philosopher Confucius, a Chinese must know 8,000 characters. Hundreds of years ago, when people took examinations to get jobs in the emperor's government, students had to know more than 10,000 characters.

These students were judged on their handwriting as well as on their answers to the test questions. Today the emperor and his examination system are long gone. However, calligraphy, the art of writing, remains very important. In many countries people such as lawyers, doctors, and business managers are not concerned about the appearance of their handwriting. But educated Chinese take pride in the clarity and beauty of their writing. The Chinese believe that because a character is a picture of an idea, the way people write tells a lot about their personalities. A bureau chief will judge the ability of an office worker by that person's calligraphy.

If you can write Chinese, you can be an artist. It is that simple. You don't have to paint mountains, carve jade, or glaze porcelain. With enough practice, a Chinese can make every written word a work of art. On page 47, Mr. Chu has written a poem by the great poet Zhang Ji, who lived in the eighth century. Can you find the characters for "mountain" and "sun" in the poem?

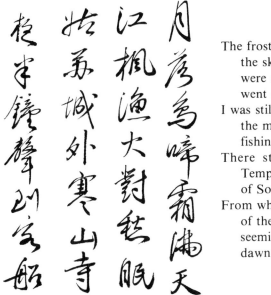

The frost was all over in
    the sky, while the crows
    were cawing as the moon
    went down.
I was still asleep, facing
    the maple leaves and
    fishing lights.
There stood the Cold-mountain
    Temple out of the city
    of Soochow;
From which the midnight booming
    of the bell came to my boat,
    seemingly telling me it was
    dawn.

An example of Chinese writing:
Copy of a poem by Zhang Ji, an eighth century Chinese poet.

Poetry has been written or printed on paper for a very long time. Did you know that the Chinese invented paper nearly two thousand years ago? Back then, when much of the Western world was ruled by the Romans, most people wrote on material made from papyrus, a reed, and on animal skins. The Chinese, however, discovered how to make paper. First they mashed bamboo plants and boiled the stalk fibers. Then they poured the mixture in a tray with a mesh bottom. When the water drained through the bottom, the thin layer of matted pulp that remained was paper.

At first paper was used only by scholars and government officials. When the Chinese discovered how to make paper in greater quantities, they used it for other things. A tough, thick paper was oiled and stretched over openings in the walls of buildings to let in light. Lanterns were made by covering a candle holder with a thinner paper. And the finest paper was used to make papercuts.

Papercuts are extremely popular in China today. Those displayed on windows are called Window Flowers—whether the designs are flowers or something else. Papercuts stuck on doorjambs are named Luck Hangings. A papercut on a door may show a woman with a broom. She is supposed to sweep away the rain and bring clear skies. Another may show a rooster, which is believed to protect the house against fire. Fans, folding screens, the corners of mirrors, and gift packages often have papercuts, too.

How are these wonderful objects made? To do a papercut at home, Chinese children buy a ready-made pattern and place it on a stack of colored papers. Then they hold the stack upside down over the smoke of an oil lamp. When the pattern is removed, a clearly marked area of unsmoked paper shows. The children cut around this.

There are also thousands of artists, known as masters, who cut freehand. They have made so many papercuts that they can follow a design on paper as if it were drawn there. The picture in their mind moves the scissors. They cut in one long, continuous motion, never stopping to go back.

When a pattern is complicated, part is cut with scissors and the rest with different sized knives, chisels, and punches. Sometimes a needle is used to make fine dotted lines and holes. The smallest designs are an inch square, and the biggest several feet square. The larger ones are cut out in sections and pasted together.

Scissors, knives, chisels, and punches are used to make the delicate papercuts.

New Year's is the most popular time for papercuts. New ones decorate the walls, doorways, and
lanterns. Papercut flags fly from the tops of cakes.
Streamers covered with papercut calligraphy swirl
along the streets. Papercuts are also the main decora-
tion for funerals, birthdays, and weddings. When the
Chinese immigrate to another country they often
bring papercuts carefully folded between layers of
clothes. The brightly-colored designs make a strange
apartment in a strange city seem more like home.

The favorite color for papercuts is red, standing
for joy and life. The traditional subjects for papercuts
include the *qi-lin*, an imaginary beast similar to a
unicorn; the lotus and pig for wealth; lions and tigers
for courage; cranes and peaches for long life; and
various Chinese characters such as "luck" and "happiness." Today political slogans such as "the great
leap forward" are also used.

Modern designs show scenes of dams and bridges
against the craggy mountains, tractors in bamboo
groves, and even apartment houses and city views.
Figures are often machinists with their tools, scien-
tists with their microscopes, and children playing
sports or helping in the fields. And as always there are
characters from Chinese opera.

In China opera is as popular as baseball and
football are in America. Every village has a stage on

which traveling opera companies perform several times a year, and every town has a theater. When the opera company comes to town, homes and teahouses are empty in the evening because people go to the opera. Larger cities such as Beijing and Shanghai have opera all year round.

Chinese opera resembles baseball and football in another way. Normally the Chinese are reserved in public. But at the opera, they cheer a good song, talk to one another about the story, and even bring food and drinks. The best seats are in front where it is easiest to hear the music. Toward the back where the cheaper seats are located, the performers must compete with lots of eating and drinking to be heard.

Everybody goes to have fun. Children are just as excited as when the circus comes to town. Chinese opera is not just singing. It includes acrobatics, dancing, fancy costumes, wild masks, and make-up as well. In some operas there is more dancing than singing. In others acrobats hold center stage. They do handsprings and cartwheels, and stand on each other's knees and shoulders to form human pyramids.

The performers use acrobatics, dancing, and other body movements to express their feelings. To express surprise, an army officer may do backward flips. A woman in danger shows her fear by shaking her head and arms like leaves blown by the wind. A husband in a rage whirls about the stage like a tornado.

The actors and actresses in the opera use only a few objects to show where events are happening. A small table becomes the royal court when the emperor stands behind it. In another scene, it is a table in a teahouse. Or two chairs may be tilted against the table to make it a mountain. Acrobats will climb all over the chairs and table to show a long journey to the

A colorfully costumed actor from one of China's touring opera companies awaits his turn to go on stage.

Dalton Delan

top of a mountain. A riding whip means someone is riding a horse. A banner means that a general is leading an army. A lantern shows that it is night.

What kind of stories do Chinese operas tell? Some operas are about myths and fairy tales. Others concern the heroic acts of modern-day Chinese citizens. Many others tell about history. Until recently, those who could not read learned about China's past through operas.

The arts in China are all deeply concerned with the past. Artistic achievements of the past move the hand that cuts the colored papers or that brushes the ink strokes of letters. Chinese artists or singers aim to equal tradition, or even better it. It would never occur to them to ignore or discount it.

4. *From Emperors to Communes*

Like many Westerners, the Chinese love history. Every Chinese student knows how General Mong Tian built the Great Wall; how Mao Zedong and his 100,000 followers marched 6,000 miles (9,600 kilometers) to escape the armies of Chiang Kai-shek.

Compared to the United States or Canada, China has a very, very long history. A Chinese student must study the people and events of 5,000 years. Think how hard it is to remember all the U.S. presidents or

Canadian prime ministers. Then guess how many emperors, presidents, and party chairmen have ruled China—over 300!

The Chinese regard their history so highly that an Official Historian was an honored person from the earliest times. His job was to write down exactly what happened. Sometimes this made an emperor angry, but the historian recorded the bad as well as the good. In hard times, his was a dangerous job!

China's history begins about 3,000 B.C.. The histories written by the earliest Official Historians tell that the first rulers were culture-heroes. They taught the people how to use fire, how to grow rice and other grains, how to read and write, and how to make silk.

These were legendary times. Rulers lived simply, and people were content. Later, emperors added a new position in the court. This was the Official Reminder. His job was to criticize government officials. He even criticized ministers and governors who lived too richly or ruled unjustly. Often the Official Reminder urged the officials to live simply like the ancients. Like the Official Historian's job, this was not work for the weak-hearted.

Until 200 B.C., China was divided into many states, each of which had its own lord. The lords bowed to the emperor but ruled their own states as they pleased. About 200 B.C., the ruler of the state of

Qin began to conquer all the other states. The Chinese said he was like a big fish who was swallowing smaller ones. This ruler's son led the army in victory after victory. The boy was only thirteen years old and very ambitious. When his father died, the young man took his place. Soon he conquered all the other states. He declared himself Qin Shi Huang, the first emperor of all China. He wore yellow robes like the legendary first rulers.

Qin Shi Huang believed that good government was harsh government. He rejected the historian's and reminder's view that he should govern gently. "Power makes right," he boasted. He even made his own mother leave his court when he found out that she had secretly married.

Court officials were shocked. Some spoke out against the emperor. They reminded him that a son must always treat a parent with respect. Twenty-seven men died for their words. Another brave court scholar, Mao Jiao, still dared to criticize the emperor. Finally Qin Shi Huang softened and brought his mother back to court.

Qin Shi Huang also kept the sons of powerful lords at his court as hostages. If a lord rebelled or refused to pay his taxes, Qin Shi Huang threatened to kill his son. The emperor sent many of his enemies and rivals to work as laborers on the Great Wall.

The Great Wall of China is the longest structure ever built. It winds nearly 4,000 miles (6,400 kilometers) across the northern part of the country.

We marvel at the length (3,900 miles; 6,240 kilometers) and height (20 to 40 feet; 6 to 12 meters) of the double wall. But in Qin Shi Huang's time, the Great Wall struck terror into the hearts of ordinary citizens. To build this barrier against the Tartar tribes, the emperor drafted hundreds of thousands of men. Many women watched their husbands and sons leave for the Great Wall and never saw them return. Only the hardiest workers could survive the blistering summer heat, the bitter winter winds, and the whip of General Mong Tian.

After Qin Shi Huang died, the Qin dynasty collapsed. Confucian scholars said that if a government ruled unfairly or stupidly, heaven withdrew its support in favor of someone else. The Han dynasty overthrew Qin Shi Huang's family and ruled from 200 B.C. to A.D. 200.

Wu Di, an early Han emperor, gave high places to the Confucian scholars that Qin Shi Huang had disliked. Wu Di began a system of examinations to select the best people to work in the government. Boys from all over China came to the capital to write their exams. Those who did well in history and poetry, and on the Confucian classics, passed the tests to enter government schools. There they learned the skills and manners becoming to an official.

Some stayed at the emperor's court and held high

positions like Official Reminder, or Minister of the Treasury. Others went to the provinces as governors, tax collectors, and judges. The officials were the emperor's hands and feet. Emperors gained power and lost power, but the official class continued to govern China until the twentieth century.

By the time of the Tang ruler, Xuan Zong (A.D. 712-756), China was the glory of the world. Persians and Japanese came to it by sea. Indians, Tibetans, and Turks came by land. China's markets were busy with people buying goods from all over the world. Xuan Zong's treasury was full of gold and silver.

The emperor spent a great amount of money on China's culture. For his Imperial Park he imported lions, bears, peacocks, and unusual plants and trees. He kept a large stable of dancing horses. These large warhorses picked up their hooves and pranced to the military music of pipes and drums. The emperor was so proud of the horses that he had one of the court's best artists paint their portraits.

Xuan Zong also brought craftspeople, poets, dancers, and singers to his court. Royal workshops hummed with the activity of potters, weavers, silversmiths, and carpenters.

As he grew older, Xuan Zong liked nothing better than to pass the evenings drinking rice wine with his poets. Gradually, the emperor let government matters slip. After sitting up all night listening to music and poetry, he was too tired to go about government business in the morning. Xuan Zong turned over this responsibility to an advisor, who filled his pockets with money at others' expense.

At the palace, poets praised wine and women, carvers made beautiful statues, and dancers entertained. But life for people in the rest of China was much less pleasant. Xuan Zong did not know that many of them had nothing to eat and were starving to death. The poet Du Fu wrote:

> From the palace gates come the smells of wine and roasts.
> In the road are bones of men who starved to death.

Nor was Xuan Zong ready for An Lu-shan. This general partied with the emperor at night, but plotted rebellion during the day. The peace-loving Xuan Zong had to flee when An Lu-shan and his army attacked the capital city.

As the emperors grew weak and the officials dishonest, foreigners came to rule China, not just to trade there. When Marco Polo arrived in Beijing in 1275, the Mongols had taken over northern China. Kublai Khan marched his army southward until the

Chinese emperor and his family faced certain capture. Rather than be disgraced as captives in Kublai Khan's court, the royal family jumped into the China Sea and drowned.

Though born on the steppes of central Asia, Kublai Khan loved China. His grandfather, Genghis Khan, swore he would never live in a walled town. But the grandson did, making the northern city of Beijing his capital.

Kublai Khan appointed many Mongols and other Turks to important positions in government. Yet the great Khan and his leaders were completely won over by Chinese culture and science. Just as Xuan Zong had encouraged poetry and painting, Kublai Khan supported the sciences. Kublai Khan passed his time at the observatory, a place for looking at the stars, discussing comets with the astronomers. He also went over plans with engineers working on the Grand Canal. Often he walked among his gardens at Xandu, where he raised rare fish and experimented with fruit trees.

Kublai Khan's empire was so safe that it was said that "a young woman carrying a gold nugget on her head can travel safely." But after the great Mongol died, the Chinese overthrew the foreign dynasty, or ruling family. The next dynasties attempted to keep out all foreigners, especially those from the West. The

Chinese assumed that they were superior to everybody else.

For this reason they were terribly shocked when British warships forced the Chinese to open their ports to traders in 1840. From 1850 to 1947, the peasants became poorer and poorer. They paid over half their crops for taxes and rent. Most landlords thought only of growing rich and doing as little work as possible. Just to buy grain to plant the next crop, peasant families had to sell their daughters and sons into slavery. When they could no longer pay their rent, peasants lost their land. Thousands and thousands of families wandered from town to town, begging for food and dying by the roadside.

In 1911 a popular revolt overthrew China's last emperor. Some years later, a young general named Chiang Kai-shek took over. He claimed to be democratic, but he ruled as a dictator and did little for the peasants. One of Chiang's partners, Mao Zedong, vowed that he would give China back to the peasants, who had toiled thousands of years for so little.

In the province of Jiangxi, Mao started a communist society. Instead of landlords, the government owned the land. It distributed food and clothes according to people's needs. Mao built schools and hospitals that were open to everyone.

This small communist state lasted until 1934,

*During World War II, Mao Zedong (left) and his troops
fought to drive the Japanese out of China. Then they battled
the Nationalist army of Chiang Kai-shek to gain control of the
country.*

when Chiang Kai-shek sent a large army to destroy the Communists. What followed is called the Long March. Fleeing from Chiang's army, Mao and 100,000 followers walked 6,000 miles (9,600 kilometers) to Yan'an on the northern border of China. Only 20,000 survived. Those who did were more committed to Mao than ever.

In Yan'an the peasants welcomed the Communists, who had to live in caves. But they survived the miserable life. After World War II, Mao marched his army to the south and defeated Chiang Kai-shek. In 1949 Mao took control of all of China except Taiwan, a large island to which Chiang retreated.

As chairman of the Communist Party, Mao cared only about one thing—revolutionizing China from top to bottom. In place of the old landlord system, he divided the countryside into communes of 2,000 families each. No longer did individuals own land. In a commune, land, buildings, and machinery belong to everyone. In old China, officials never did hand labor. Mao made everyone till the land or work in a factory. In the days of the emperors, only the scholars could read and write. Now all girls and boys went to school. Before the Communists gained power, you could tell what rank a person had by his or her clothes. Mao made everybody—women included— wear the same plain outfits.

As time passed, Mao feared that the spirit that helped his followers survive the Long March and reform people's way of living would die. In 1966 he began what he called the Cultural Revolution. Led by Mao's wife, Jiang Qing, groups of students attacked party leaders, teachers, and factory managers for being lazy and old-fashioned. Thousands of national and community leaders lost their jobs. Many had to stand before large crowds and confess their mistakes.

For several years, the Cultural Revolution disrupted everything. Factories fell idle, schools closed their doors, and people lived in fear. Mao watched from a distance. In his study, he wrote poetry and essays. He heard reports that leaders of the Cultural Revolution were punishing innocent people. But when he appeared in public, he praised the "clean sweep."

Mao died in 1976. He was one of the great leaders of the modern world. He led China from weakness to strength, from despair to hope. He gave China back to her people.

The new government after Mao stopped the Cultural Revolution. It called Mao's widow, Jiang Qing, and three other leaders of the Cultural Revolution — Wang Hongwen, Yao Wenyuan, and Zhang Chunqiao — the "Gang of Four." They were arrested and put on trial.

The court found the Gang of Four guilty of hurting many innocent people. It sentenced Jiang Qing and Zhang Chunqiao to die, Wang Hongwen to be jailed for life, and Yao Wenyuan to spend twenty years in prison. Government leaders later allowed Jiang and Zhang to live, but kept them in jail.

Since Jiang's fall from power, China's new leaders have been changing many of the policies the country followed under Mao Zedong. They want the government to play a smaller role in the economy and have allowed communes and factories greater freedom in making and selling products. Communes have even been permitted to sell some of their crops for a profit.

The government has also been increasing trade and contacts with other countries. It is especially interested in obtaining help and advice in making China's industry and agriculture more modern. In some cases, foreign companies have been asked to build new factories in China. Chinese students have also been sent to Western schools to receive advanced scientific and technical training.

China's leaders are very worried about their country's future. At a recent meeting of the Chinese Communist Party, these leaders spoke out against selfish behavior, dishonesty, and crime. The chairman of the party, Hu Yaobang, said that if China does not overcome these problems, it cannot reach its goal of becoming a more modern nation.

Hu also said that many Chinese have lost their belief in the ideals that once moved the country forward. Too many people, he stated, are only looking out for themselves, instead of working for the common good. In addition, he pointed out that dishonesty in government, crime, and drug abuse are on the rise.

One reason for these problems is that some government officials have not set a good example for the people. These officials sometimes break the law by accepting money or goods to do special favors for someone. For example, a grocery store in Fushan had to supply local political leaders with liquor, tobacco, and pork to obtain extra gasoline and to keep its building maintained.

Ordinary Chinese resent this type of behavior. As James Kenneson, an American who recently lived in China, puts it, "When [common] people see party members and [officials] doing next to nothing while living in the best apartments, eating the best food, getting the best cloth, . . . and sending their children to the best schools, they tend to get upset. Unable to express [resentment, they] simply do less work."

Party officials are especially worried about China's young men and women. The party's journal, *The*

Red Flag, estimates that nearly one out of every three young workers has no goals or sense of purpose. As a result, it says, they " 'lead lives devoid of [, or lacking in,] meaning.' "

Hu Yaobang blames the younger workers' attitudes on the poor education they received during the ten years of the Cultural Revolution. Schools were often closed in this period, and many young people did not learn enough to become productive workers. Today these young adults "regard themselves as members of a lost generation . . . [who have] little prospect for advancement."

Faced with this situation, the Communist Party has begun a campaign to give new life to its ideals and to stamp out dishonesty and crime. Within the next five years, the party wants to see " 'markedly better public order, generally improved attitudes towards all types of work, and a conspicuous [, or noticeable,] decline in the crime rate.' "

The party has also taken steps to change its own structure. Party leaders want to reduce the influence that Mao Zedong's ideas still have on China and to open the way for younger leaders to come into power. Under a new constitution that the Communists have adopted, many of the most important positions in the party will be done away with. Chief among these positions is the post of party chairman, which had

Dalton Delan

China's schools were often closed during the ten years of the Cultural Revolution. Now classes are being held once again, and students often march out to visit farms and factories as part of their education.

been created for Mao Zedong. In addition, older members of the party will be urged to take a less active role in its affairs. Finally, all 39 million Chinese who have been admitted to the party will have to meet stricter membership standards.

These changes in the Communist Party have been brought about largely because of the influence of Deng Xiaoping, China's most important leader. He plans to resign his position as deputy chairman of the party, but he will continue to maintain his authority. Deng has also seen to it that Hu Yaobang will not lose any power in moving from chairman to general secretary of the Communist Party.

What will happen to China as it seeks to become a more modern nation is difficult to say. Most of the country's people appear to support the Communist leaders, though, and this support is essential to any plans party officials may make. For the people are China's greatest resource, and its future depends on their attitudes, energies, and abilities.

5. A Treasure in Words

Wonderful stories are often set in beautiful, imaginary places, such as the Emerald City in the Land of Oz. Many of the stories the Chinese love are set in Hangzhou, a real city in southeastern China. More than two thousand years old, it is a marvelous sight to behold. Once the capital of the ancient Song emperors, it has a great number of lovely gardens, statues, and temples.

On holidays, the Chinese sometimes travel to

Hangzhou's West Lake, where they rent boats and explore the shore. Later they have something to eat or drink in the ancient pavilions near the lake that have been made into public cafés.

Even on a hot afternoon, the stone floor of these buildings, worn shiny with the years, feels cool underneath your feet. The café-goers relax in curved cane armchairs, and sip tea from porcelain mugs. Sometimes, towards late afternoon, they begin to tell folktales about imaginary beings in China's distant past. One of these tales, "Bright Pearl," explains how West Lake was made.

Long ago, in a cave east of the Milky Way, there lived a snow-white jade dragon. West of the Milky Way, in a big forest, dwelled a gold phoenix. The two were neighbors, and every morning they came out to greet each other. The dragon swished hello with his tail, and the phoenix cocked her head in reply. Then they each hurried off to do the day's work.

One day, when the phoenix was flying in the sky and the dragon was swimming in the Milky Way, they discovered a fairy island. On it was a bright, shiny stone. "Look, Jade Dragon! What a beautiful stone!" said the phoenix, calling to her friend. The dragon admired it, too. "Shall we work on it and make it into a pearl?"

The gold phoenix nodded her head, and they

started to work on it. They sprinkled it with dew from the fairy mountain and pure water from the Milky Way. They worked on the stone day after day and year after year, turning it into a bright pearl.

The dragon and the phoenix cherished this pearl. Soon they discovered that they also loved each other. As a result, they had no desire to return to their old homes. Instead, they stayed on the fairy island and watched over the pearl day and night.

One day the Queen Mother of the West walked out of her palace gate and saw the pearl's beaming light. She thought it was so fine that she ordered one of her soldiers to go and steal it. While the jade dragon and the gold phoenix were sleeping, the heavenly soldier took the pearl away, and the queen hid it in her palace. She never let anyone see it, closing it behind nine gates that were locked with nine locks.

One day, to celebrate her birthday, the Queen Mother gave an "Immortal Peach Party" for all the gods. They were all drinking wine, eating the immortal peaches, and bellowing a happy birthday song when the queen said, "My friends. I am going to show you a precious pearl, the likes of which you'll find neither in heaven nor on earth." Then she brought out the pearl on a gold platter and placed it in the middle of the big hall. The pearl gave out a shimmering beam of light.

Many Chinese stories deal with a goddess (top) or a phoenix (bottom). In "Bright Pearl," a selfish goddess steals a beautiful pearl from a phoenix and a dragon.

Meanwhile, the gold phoenix and the jade dragon looked everywhere for their pearl—high in the Milky Way and low under the fairy island. "Jade dragon!" the phoenix cried out when he saw the shining light. "Hurry and look. Isn't that light in the sky from our pearl?"

"You're right," answered the dragon. "It must be our pearl. Let's hurry and get it back."

They rushed to the palace of the Queen of the West just as the gods were praising the splendid pearl. When they asked the queen for their pearl, she flew into a rage, saying "What nonsense! All heaven's treasures belong to me!" But the dragon and phoenix became angry, too, and the dragon's reply was fiery when he shouted back: "This pearl was not born of heaven nor grown on earth. We two ground it and pecked it out with much hard work."

The queen ordered her generals to drive away the visitors. When the gold phoenix saw that the queen was going to be so unfair, she rushed forward to grab the pearl. So did the jade dragon and the queen. Soon three pairs of hands were tugging at the gold platter, and none of them would let go. The platter swayed and tipped and the bright pearl rolled off, falling down the stairs from heaven towards the earth.

The dragon and phoenix caught up with their pearl and danced along on either side to protect it.

Slowly it fell to earth. No sooner did it touch the ground than it became the West Lake.

Neither the dragon nor the phoenix could bear the thought of leaving their pearl. The dragon turned into the high Jade Dragon Mountain to shield the pearl, and the gold phoenix turned into the green Phoenix Mountain to guard the pearl from the other side. And ever since these two mountains have been quietly standing beside West Lake.

A Famous Character

Four hundred years ago a Chinese writer, Wu Cheng-en, wrote down all the ghost and folk stories he loved as a child into a big book. He wove them into a long adventure story about Monkey, a fearless character who performs godlike feats. It is a book of wise nonsense and daring deeds which has delighted millions of Chinese children and adults to this very day.

The first part of the story shows how Monkey spent twenty years serving a holy man who taught him magic powers, such as how to change shapes and fly in the air. Then he spent time in heaven, eating Immortal Peaches, drinking Heavenly Wine, and taking the Elixir of Long Life. His rebellious behavior often angered the other gods. That first half of the story is called "Havoc in Heaven." In the second part, Monkey goes with a monk to obtain some sacred religious writings.

Few works of ancient Chinese literature were printed during the Cultural Revolution, but the book about Monkey was an exception. It has even come out as a long comic book and as a feature cartoon.

Proverbs

Fortune cookies were the invention of a chef in a Chinese restaurant in San Francisco in the 1920s. They were unknown in old China. What inspired him were Chinese proverbs. The papers in the cookies seldom predict anything. They remind people how to act in the present to prepare themselves for a good future.

In China, everyone uses proverbs. They are the shortcuts of everyday speech. After learning to write single characters, students move on to writing proverbs in their second grade copybooks. Proverbs save arguments and solve problems because they have the weight and authority of the past. No Chinese person would say, "You should think before you speak." They would say instead, "Think three times, then do it."

The advice Chinese proverbs give is very direct

and often humorous. Some of them stress respect for old people, loyalty to friends, and cheerfulness. Others are concerned with business, eating and drinking, and wealth and poverty. Two very well-known proverbs compare human behavior to the cooking of rice. You would never find them in a fortune cookie in America, though, because they need an explanation.

"Even a clever daughter-in-law can't cook without rice" goes the first. This proverb means that without the right tools, even the greatest skill is useless. The word-picture is more colorful than saying, "You cannot make something out of nothing."

The other famous rice proverb is even briefer: "The rice has been cooked." This saying means that there are many decisions in life which cannot be changed. For as the Chinese well know, once rice is cooked it can never be made hard again.

Here are a few of the other bits of Chinese folk wisdom that deal with rice. They come from south of the Yangzi River, the rice-eating half of China.

"Drawing pictures of rice cakes won't stop hunger." (If you really want something, you must work hard for it.)

"If you eat his rice, you must obey him." (Like it or not, you must take orders from your boss.)

"Every ladle strikes the edge of the rice pot once

in a while." (Even the best of families have disagreements.)

These proverbs, along with the tales of dragons and monkeys, are only a small part of China's treasure in words. For the Chinese have been expressing themselves in stories and sayings for thousands of years. They have written and spoken about many things, and yet, as this chapter shows, they have long given an important place to beauty, humor, and wisdom.

6. Holidays:
Old and New

It is Chinese New Year in Canton. Groups of girls and boys dressed in brightly-colored quilted jackets and trousers dance through a sea of exploding fire-crackers. Some grown-ups cover their ears, and some small children cry. But the festive lion never flinches. Its mouth gaping and its eyes rolling toward heaven, the marvelous beast ranges from one side of the street to the other.

　　In front of the lion runs the teaser, announcing its

arrival. He wears a pumpkinlike mask and carries a fireball baton. To the rear, a band of marchers plays cymbals, gongs, and a huge kettle drum pulled on a wagon.

Chinese New Year is a time of renewal and good fortune. To receive the lion's favor and good luck for the rest of the year, people hold out cabbages to the beast as it passes by. Prancing with its head held high, the lion swirls around the gift. Then it bobs low to the ground and sweeps the cabbage into its mouth.

In former times, the new year holiday fell between mid-January and the end of February, on the first day of the first month of the old lunar calendar. Now that the People's Republic goes by the same calendar as the West, however, the new year actually begins on January 1. The old holiday is now called the Spring Festival, but it is still celebrated on the same date.

Preparations for the holiday begin a week before it takes place. Among other things, the Chinese scrub their homes, factories, shops, and communes. Once the new year festivities start, cleaning is not permitted until the celebration ends. People believe so much luck arrives with the new year that cleaning during the celebration might sweep or wash some of it away. Some Canton families even put away their knives and scissors for fear that someone might cut the new year's good luck in two.

On New Year's Eve, the people of Shanghai decorate their homes with red paper signs saying Peace, Good Health, Prosperity, and Houseful of Blessings. The words *Always Full* go on the rice bin; *In and Out in Peace* on doors. Some families seal their doors with strips of red paper that are not broken until the following day.

The last meal of the old year is called the Join Together or Reunion Dinner. The larger family, including grandparents, aunts, uncles, and cousins, gathers at a great feast. They cannot eat everything that is prepared, though. There must be enough food for leftovers, which are considered lucky and are eaten the next day.

At the New Year's Eve meal, young and old stand up and play games while they are eating. Children enjoy Rock, Scissors, Paper, which was invented in the Far East and is played worldwide. The winner eats from the loser's plate of food. Adults play a similar game in which two persons flash fingers, each guessing how many fingers the other will extend. Later some people join the crowds in the streets, while others stay at home to play cards or talk until dawn.

New Year's morning, children wake up early and wish their parents *Gong ho xin xi,* or "Respectful greetings, new happiness." The parents give each child a red and gold envelope of "lucky money."

Children may spend this money as they wish or save it. A child who can visit grandparents, uncles, or aunts on New Year's Day will also usually receive little envelopes of lucky money from them.

During the day, people either make visits or stay home to receive guests. Visitors bring presents of sweets, lichee nuts, and kumquats. Guests drink tea sweetened with Chinese red dates, and eat bite-sized turnovers filled with spicy meat as well as fried dumplings flaked with sesame seeds. Large, round Cantonese-style loaves of carrot cake, cut into small pieces, are also popular. Happy New Year is written on top of the cake in red food coloring. Some people try to make their visits in such a way that their path forms a circle, because the Chinese word for this shape also sounds like the one for good luck.

The Chinese do not have to work or attend school for the first three days of the new year. People in Canton go to movies and to operas. The operas feature costume dramas about life in China during the Middle Ages and in the China of today. They also attend events like martial arts demonstrations and folk dances. Stilt-walking and riddles are especially popular with children at New Year's.

In the countryside of north and northeast China, people make *nian hua,* new year pictures. This folk art has been done for a thousand years. Its center is in

Festive dances are performed on many Chinese holidays, including the New Year's celebration.

Weifang, a town in Shangdong Province. Millions of Chinese buy the pictures that are made in this town.

The walls, windows, and doors of every workshop in Weifang and nearby villages are decorated with the colorful and lively nian hua. Some show a traditional scene, such as *The Mouse's Wedding*. Others have big flowers such as peonies, lotuses, plum blossoms, and camellias. Some pictures come in pairs: for example, a girl carrying a shovel to the fields, and a young worker with pliers in his hand watching his machine. Blazing red and yellow are the favorite colors. And the pictures are shaped and sized to fit any space where people might want to use them—on gates, doors, screen walls, windows, and carts; over beds; even in pigsties.

People paste the pictures on both the front and back door. On either side of a pair of door pictures, someone handwrites a poem. The characters for the word *happiness* go over the door, and a row of papercuts hangs between them. Door pictures used to be put up to chase away the evil spirits, but today most Chinese appreciate them only as good traditional art.

Qing Ming

In early April the Chinese have their *Qing Ming* ("Tomb Sweeping") or Pure Brightness Festival. At this time they visit the graves of their ancestors, relatives, and friends. In olden times, they brought along sprigs of willow, incense, paper money, and paper models of things they thought their forebears needed. They swept the graves and placed sacrifices on them in a formal ceremony. Then they gathered for a holiday meal.

Qing Ming is no longer treated so seriously. There is not a formal ceremony at the gravesite, and after the tombs are swept and the incense burned, the meal begins. In Beijing, Qing Ming comes at the beginning of lovely spring weather. It is a day on which thousands of men, women, and children participate in foot races.

International Workers Day

Like most communist countries, the People's Republic celebrates a day for workers on May 1. Throughout China there are official gatherings for people who labor on communes and in factories. Flags, banners, and posters praising the workers are put up where everyone can see them. Dances and plays are rehearsed for the occasion, and there are organized athletic events in squares and on playing fields.

Government heads join the people in watching

public performances. Some people spend the day working on their private plots of land or doing some type of creative art or music. Many city families take day trips to the countryside. The day ends with dancing and fireworks.

Mid-Autumn Festival

On the fifteenth day of the eighth moon of the old lunar calendar comes the most romantic Chinese celebration, the Mid-Autumn or Moon Festival. On this night the full moon is supposed to shine brighter than at any other time of the year. People buy "moon cakes" at pastry shops and bring them to relatives and friends in small boxes tied with ribbons. These cakes, baked of "moon-colored" or gray flour, are sweet and sugary, and loaded with spices, orange peel, almonds, nuts, and fruit.

On the night of the festival, families and friends gather together for a feast. Those who have roof gardens give moon-viewing parties, and the parks and resort cafés are filled with people who like their banquet out-of-doors.

Moon cakes are important symbols for the Mid-Autumn Festival. According to one legend, some six hundred years ago the cakes helped the Chinese to overthrow the Tartars, a group of fierce Turkish warriors who had conquered their country. Very secretly, the Chinese decided that the overthrow would take place at the time of the Moon Festival. On the eve of the festival, moon cakes were given from friend to friend, as usual. But inside each cake was the same note: "Kill the Tartars in your house tonight!" This trick helped the Chinese destroy the Tartar rule.

National Day

The Chinese are given two days off from work or school to celebrate National Day, which is observed on October 1. Like May Day, the accent of this holiday is on public celebration, not family parties, because it is a serious political occasion. It marks the day Mao Zedong made his triumphal entrance into Beijing with his army in 1949.

On National Day there are great marches through the streets, which are bright with banners and strings of colored lights. People dress in their best clothes, special dishes are prepared, and cities hold huge public rallies.

A favorite display at the rallies is "placard art," which is performed in sports stadiums by several thousand people. Each person who participates has a stack of colored cards. When a signal is given, he or she holds up one of these cards, or placards, to help

Thousands of people help to create the beautiful placard art that is displayed in sports stadiums on National Day.

make a picture. The person may put up the black pupil of the Chinese premier's eye for one picture, and a chrysanthemum petal for the next.

Not only are big portraits and still objects made this way, but even huge birds that appear to fly across the stadium. The stadium is so large and the cards so small that you don't see the individual pieces, just the overall pattern. Everyone must perform on time for the picture to be successful.

Holidays for Women and Children

The Chinese have special days to honor women and children. Instead of Mother's Day, they honor all women on International Working Women's Day, March 8. Children give their mothers small gifts such as teamats and papercuts they have made themselves. Workplaces give all women a half-day off. Speakers recall the hard life women led in imperial China and honor the achievements of women today.

Children's Day, June 1, is a time for games and festivities at school. Students run relay races, take part in tugs-of-war, play Chinese chess, and try to take marbles from a china bowl using chopsticks. The children also present ballets, puppet shows, and plays they have written themselves.

Some children become members of the Young

Children's Day gives students a chance to exhibit their special talents. These kindergarten-age girls are entertaining a Beijing audience with a dance.

Pioneers, China's major youth organization, on this day. An old member places a red scarf around the neck of the new member, while each salutes the other by raising his or her right arm.

In the afternoon, organized gymnastics exhibitions are given in town gymnasiums. Red banners are hung everywhere, and thousands of schoolchildren attend. The huge display combines traditional and Western gymnastic feats: acrobatics on the ground; exercises done on a wooden beam and the horse; Chinese boxing; and saber dances.

Like many other Chinese holidays, Children's Day is a joyous celebration filled with a variety of activities. Like them, too, it is a mixture of old and new. But that is what we should expect in a country that has been celebrating special days for thousands of years.

7. *Life on a Commune*

China has many large and famous cities. Of its nearly one billion people, though, four out of five live in rural areas. Their business is raising food. In 1958 Mao Zedong announced the Great Leap Forward. To him this program meant a rapid change to a new communist type of society. An important part of this change was the setting up of large communes in the countryside.

Before the revolution that occurred in 1949, a

small fraction of the people owned most of the land in China. These landlords were very powerful and controlled the lives of thousands of families. Although some of these landowners were just, the system itself was not. The people who actually worked the land had to give as much as half of what they grew to the landlord as rent. Because they did not own their land, most farmers had to work very hard just to survive.

In 1958 Mao took most of the land away from private owners and gave it to communes. A commune is a community that works together and then shares what it grows or makes. The people on a commune may grow wheat, raise hogs, or produce silk. Individual familes on a commune own their clothes, furniture, housewares, and other personal goods. Often they also own a small vegetable garden. But the rest of the land belongs to the commune.

Farmers work as members of large teams. By working with other families, the farmers can afford fertilizer, tractors, irrigation pumps, and other equipment. Before the revolution, families tried to farm their land without any outside help. Two families with small plots of land would each own a cow to do the plowing. One cow would have been enough to plow both fields, but the separate families had no way of sharing ownership. Today's communes allow families to share.

These commune workers are inspecting the growth of silk-worms, which feed on mulberry leaves.

In the old landowning system, most of what the farmers produced went to people who did not work. But in Communist China, everybody works. In addition, a commune first grows enough food to support itself, and then sells anything extra—its surplus—to government stores in the cities. The profits are used to buy machines that enable workers to grow more food. The government pays commune workers wages plus allowances for family expenses. Part of the money that a commune makes by selling its surplus to the government goes into higher wages.

For hundreds of years, the Chinese believed that five generations of the same family should live together. Each time a son married, he brought his wife into the family. A daughter, on the other hand, moved in with her husband's family when she married.

Under the commune system, fewer people from the same family live together. In fact, when people learn new skills they are often given jobs far from their first home. Similarly, when mothers are at their jobs, the youngest children in a family go to a day-care center.

Family life is still important to the Chinese, though. A commune cottage often shelters three generations of a family. And when holidays occur, family members who have moved away usually return home.

Families that work and produce together also share many conveniences and activities. For example, their commune may have a recreation room and a place for crafts and sewing that everyone can use. In a poor commune, even running water is shared, as are showers and toilets. This way everyone can satisfy his or her basic needs.

China has 50,000 communes in all, most of which have 10,000 or more people. They are so large that they have their own schools, health clinics, repair shops, and cultural centers. As we saw in chapter one, before the revolution most people did not have enough food. Today, many communes produce more food than they need, so that surpluses are typical, not unusual.

In the far north of China, in the province of Heilongjiang, the Chinese discovered oil in 1959. Many workers moved up there to dig oil wells and build pipelines. To feed and support these workers, their wives started a commune. The land is fertile in this area, but the growing season is short. As a result, the women knew that to turn the grasslands into fields of wheat and vegetables, they would have to work together.

At first the work went quite slowly. Since the women had no draft animals, they harnessed themselves to a plow. In that year, 1962, they cultivated only five acres. Two years later, with 300 households working, they were able to farm one hundred acres.

The women named their commune *Chuang Ye* meaning "Something From Nothing." By 1975 Chuang Ye had grown to 700 households. The women farmed 500 acres (200 hectares) and produced 225 tons of wheat, 550 tons of vegetables, and 7 tons of meat. All the things in this fine harvest had come about because a group of women agreed to work hard together!

Living on a commune is hard work. Everyone

Heavy stone walls keep a small stream within its banks at a mountain commune in Sichuan Province.

works six days a week, and even on Sunday there is usually something that has to be done. The time to relax is at meals, especially lunch or dinner. After long hours of hard work, everybody is hungry, and nobody enjoys good food more than the Chinese.

The Chinese eat rice or some other grain at every meal. In the north, people eat wheat, millet, or corn, while in the south, they eat rice. Chinese meals do not differ as much as those in most Western nations. Especially on the communes, about the same food is eaten in the morning, at midday, and in the evening.

A typical meal consists of rice and vegetables, and perhaps some chicken or meat. People often have a soup containing noodles or dumplings. At each meal the Chinese like cooked food that is served warm. Usually they drink hot tea, too, a custom that has spread all over the world. The English word *tea* comes from the Chinese word *cha*.

Perhaps you would like to try some Chinese food. Here is a recipe for making tea and Chinese vegetables to serve with rice.

Green Tea

ceramic pot
green tea (loose, not bags, from a gourmet
    foods shop)

Bring to boil two cups of water in a kettle. Meanwhile swish lots of hot water from the tap into the teapot in order to warm it. Sprinkle one teaspoon of tea (no more!) into the pot, and as soon as the water boils, fill the pot. Put the lid on the pot and let the tea inside sit for three minutes before serving it. Serves four.

Mixed Vegetables

   1 cup bean sprouts
   1 medium carrot
   1 small cucumber
   2 cups lettuce or Chinese cabbage
   1/2 cup fresh bamboo shoots (you may substitute
     canned)
   1 tablespoon cooking oil
   1 teaspoon sugar
   1 tablespoon soy sauce
   2 tablespoons water
   1/2 cup water chestnuts
   frying pan
   cooking oil

Peel cucumber. Cut all fresh vegetables, except the bean sprouts, into thin slices about 1-1/2 inches long. Slice the canned water chestnuts. Mix water, sugar, and soy sauce. Heat frying pan very hot, and add oil.

Add water mixture and vegetables. Cook for two or three minutes, stirring all the time. Serve hot with rice. Serves four.

As you can see from this recipe, ordinary Chinese meals are very simple and low in fats. The Chinese do not drink milk or eat milk products rich in fat such as butter and cheese. The only exception is that during the summer ice cream—a foreign food—is beginning to be sold in the big cities. For the most part, Chinese say that cow's milk is for baby cows. Bean curd gives them the same nutrients, or food value, that Westerners get from milk.

The Chinese eat rice the way other people eat bread. In fact, they do very little baking. Instead, they cook almost everything on their stoves. Chinese food is usually steamed, boiled, sautéed, or fried.

People in China like their food very fresh. In the commune, it is easy to find fresh vegetables, fruits, eggs, and meat. In the cities, shoppers must buy these things every day or two. The Chinese have no frozen foods and eat almost nothing from a can. They say that fresh food tastes much better.

Before the food is cooked, it is usually cut into small pieces. Chinese cooks have separate, exact ways of chopping a turnip, a cabbage leaf, or a piece of chicken. And knives never leave the kitchen.

Tasty foods can be bought at the street kitchens that are found in many Chinese cities.

At the table everyone eats with a spoon and chop-sticks. These slender wooden sticks are used in place of forks. It is really not hard to eat with them once you've had a little practice. If you go to a Chinese restaurant, you can try them for yourself. It is fun to have your own special pair!

During most of the year, Chinese food is simple. But on special occasions, such as New Year's or a wedding, the Chinese prepare huge banquets of many different dishes.

One favorite is duck. The Chinese say that they eat every part of the duck except its quack. They boil it, broil it, stuff it, and roast it. They cook the liver wrapped in the webbing of the duck's feet. They eat duck eggs that are one hundred days old. However, because they are black from being soaked in lime, salt, and tea, some people call them One-Hundred-Year-Old Eggs. Red Cooked Duck gets its color from soy sauce. Eight Precious Duck is stuffed with eight tasty ingredients such as ginger, lotus seeds, gingko nuts, and bamboo shoots.

The Chinese also enjoy sea snails, cloud ears (a gray fungus that grows on trees), bean curd, and shark fin soup. For extraspecial events, they serve bird's nest soup. The key element in this dish comes from the nest of the swallow.

Swallows build their nests on the side of a steep

cliff, using sticky saliva to hold pieces of grass and twigs together. To make bird's nest soup, someone has to climb up the cliff and take the nest. Afterwards it is carefully soaked in water to loosen the sticky net that holds it together. This net is then cooked with vegetables and spices to make the soup.

Here are two special dishes for you to make. The main dish is served with rice. *Foo yung* means "mimosa flower," the shape the egg takes when it is cooked.

Egg Foo Yung

     1 cup canned crabmeat
     1 slice (about a teaspoon) ginger root
     6 eggs
     1/2 teaspoon salt
     frying pan
     cooking oil

Cut the ginger root into bits. Drain the crabmeat, remove any bone, and cut up. Beat eggs lightly with salt, crabmeat, and ginger root. Heat small frying pan very hot. Add two tablespoons cooking oil. Spoon one-third of the egg mixture into the oil. Fry at medium heat until crisp (about two minutes). Tilt the pan to let uncooked part run to sides. Flip with a spatula and brown the other side. Cook the thin egg pancakes one at a time. Keep them hot on a pieplate in the oven until all are done and the sauce is ready. Serves three.

Sauce for Egg Foo Yung

3/4 cup canned beef broth
2 tablespoons soy sauce
1 teaspoon sugar
1/4 cup bamboo shoots
6 water chestnuts
1 tablespoon each water and cornstarch mixed

Cut the bamboo shoots into small pieces and slice the chestnuts. Bring the broth mixture to the boiling point and then reduce heat. Add cornstarch mixture. Stir a minute or two until sauce is thick. Pour sauce over the foo yung and serve. Serves three.

Simpler dishes must be served on working days. Almost everybody in China wakes up at six in the morning and starts work by seven. Commune workers go to the fields even earlier. After a long morning's work, they have lunch, the big meal of the day. Then they return to their jobs for several more hours. In the evening, everyone has a light supper.

The Chinese always try to eat together. Mealtime gives them a chance to enjoy other people. On the commune, it is also a time to make plans and discuss problems.

When Mao Zedong took over China, there was starvation everywhere. Today the communes grow enough food for themselves and for people in the city. As a result, mealtime can be the happy occasion that the Chinese like it to be.

Not everyone in China likes the commune system. But it has given millions of Chinese a better life. For under this system land has been more fairly distributed, work more evenly divided, and profits more widely shared. Now people no longer need to pay enormous rents or become beggars. Instead, they can work together for the common good, knowing that their basic needs for food, clothing, and shelter will be satisfied.

8. *Learning to Serve the People*

Ha O Lin is an eleven-year-old girl in Shanghai who is in her last year of middle school. She lives in a small three-room apartment with her mother, father, grandmother, and older brother. Her older brother, Ha Wang Chu, is in high school, and her mother and father, who work in a nearby metal factory, are both chemistry students at college.

Ha O Lin is one of about 210 million students who attend elementary and secondary schools in

China. About 150 million of the students are enrolled in elementary schools, which are free to everyone. They begin going at the age of six or seven and stay for five years. Afterwards, like Ha O Lin, they may enter secondary or middle schools and study for another five years. Nearly 60 million youngsters attend these schools, where they pay a small fee for tuition and buy their own books and supplies.

China has 675 universities and technical colleges, with just over a million students. This figure means that one in twenty people go on to a university after completing middle school. Before they enter college, however, they do practical farm work for two years or more. Many go from the big cities to remote areas like Inner Mongolia, Tibet, and the southwestern parts of China.

University programs emphasize farming, industry, and government. A good record for the years of farm work, along with good reports from others on the work team, qualifies students for the university. Before they enroll, they must also pass an entrance examination. If they are successful, they will receive a free college education.

Many students are in their late twenties or thirties by the time they begin their studies. Those who have children receive full pay during their college years. Nevertheless, all students must continue to do some practical work because government officials don't want them to live and think too much differently than ordinary working people. Even their classes take them out into workshops and fields.

Ha O Lin hasn't given much thought to college yet. She is too occupied with the busy life of a middle school student. She goes to school six days a week, ten months a year, with a month's vacation in the summer and another month off at New Year's.

Her day begins early, at 6:00 A.M. Before breakfast, she and her brother do exercises with the other children in the neighborhood along the street in front of their house. Then she dresses for school, putting on a printed blouse, a plum-colored jacket, gray trousers, socks, and black canvas shoes. She arrives at school just before 7:30 A.M., joining the other one thousand students who attend it. All of them live within a five-minute walk of the school grounds.

Before the bell rings to go inside, Ha O Lin lines up to learn cartwheels in the schoolyard. Children all over China are doing much the same thing at this hour.

Old and plain, Ha O Lin's schoolhouse is typical of those found in China. Clusters of small buildings, each with six classrooms, surround a central courtyard. The rooms open onto the courtyard, with no space wasted on hallways. To go from one room to the next, students have to go outside first.

Most of the courtyards are playgrounds, but one is a garden—a small farm in the middle of a big city! Here children raise eggplants, tomatoes, cucumbers, sunflowers, sugar cane, string beans, onions, peanuts, watermelon, corn, and herbs. Most of these products go into school lunches. The rest are given to the children to take home and enjoy with their families.

School is quite formal. The fifty students in each classroom sit at double desks and keep their hands clasped during lessons. When called upon, they stand to answer the teacher's question. Often, when the entire class has memorized the lesson, all the students answer together.

Along with the other pupils in her class, Ha O Lin studies the Chinese language, arithmetic, singing, art, government, and general knowledge. This last subject combines science, geography, and history.

Language study takes up as much as half of the school timetable. Learning Chinese script takes about two years longer than learning a language that is written in an alphabet. By the end of this year, Ha O Lin will know 2,000 characters, enough for reading basic Chinese. In addition, she studies Pinyin, an alphabetical way of writing Chinese that is being taught in China today to help everyone pronounce Mandarin the same. The government wants everyone to be able to read and write. Now only about two out

Most Chinese schools are old, plain-looking, and crowded. Students usually sit at double desks and pay close attention to their teachers.

of three Chinese can do these things, although there are not many people less than fifty years old who cannot.

Children in China learn to do their arithmetic with the help of an abacus, a simple, wooden, hand-operated computer. Every class in Ha O Lin's school has one, and students can do addition, multiplication, and division on it with lightning fast speed. Sometimes Ha O Lin's fingers seem to fly over the wooden beads on the abacus faster than she can think!

Art lessons emphasize the importance of picturing scenes, objects, and people from everyday life. Today in drawing class Ha O Lin copied a sunflower sitting in a vase on the teacher's desk. She used tempera paints and worked slowly and carefully. She is also learning how to write Chinese characters with a brush and ink. Calligraphy, or beautiful writing, is an ancient art form in China.

Ha O Lin began three of her courses just last year in fourth grade. They are government, English, and general knowledge.

Government, or political studies, teaches the traditions of the Communist Revolution. Students think about how to "serve the people," and how to act together as a group.

In today's English class Ha O Lin was tested on new words about the harvest. *Rice, cotton, goose/geese, cut, pick, busy, sheep, yellow,* and *pig* were the ten words she was asked to spell.

Of all the subjects Ha O Lin studies, general knowledge is the most important, because it links school with the world of work. In most western nations, school prepares students to be useful to society when they grow up. The Chinese, on the other hand, want children to do work that is useful to society while they are still in school. They also think that many important skills are best learned on the job, rather than in the classroom.

To combine school with work, students are given a course in general knowledge that helps them learn the skills that make for *laodong*, or "productive labor." This course takes place in the classroom as well as on farms and factories. Students are also taught that laodong is to be practiced out of school, even on vacations.

The idea that everyone should learn to do practical work makes Chinese schools very different from those in North America. From the age of ten, every Chinese student learns to handle machinery in the school workshop, and even nursery school children cultivate a little garden.

The activity that goes on in the workshop is not a game. The students actually make metal filters that are used by factories in the production of tractors.

The factories supply machinery, tools, materials, and even the teacher. They also have the students visit the assembly plant so that the youngsters can understand the part their work plays.

Half a day a week Ha O Lin's class goes to one of Shanghai's beautiful parks to plant, prune, weed, or clean litter. Many of China's parks are maintained by student labor.

School-run workshops teach all Chinese students ten and over how to operate and repair machinery.

Since third grade, Ha O Lin has gone on a number of field trips to a large commune on the outskirts of the city. This commune produces fruits and vegetables. Here she works side by side with farmers and learns to appreciate hand labor. Last summer she stayed at the commune for a whole week. Her class helped build wheelbarrows and repair a plow.

Ha O Lin's favorite part of the general knowledge course at the school is learning about herbs. Today her teacher showed the class how to recognize herbs that make medicines. She said, "Use your fingers as well as your eyes!" A few of the herbs are growing in pots in the school garden. Each herb is in a separate pot, and it is carefully labeled so that everybody can learn its name.

Ha O Lin has to work hard at school and do up to three hours of homework at night. She belongs to a study group organized by her school. The five children in it all live on the same street and are in the same grade. The teachers encourage the children to help one another with their assignments. One of the children acts as group leader. This person's job is to see that everyone knows what the homework is and finishes it.

Despite all the studying, Ha O Lin takes good care of her eyes. At her school, few children wear eyeglasses. Twice a day classes are interrupted for five minutes of eye exercises. The children press and rub points near the eye, brow, face, and neck. They do this repeatedly and in a precise rhythm. It is reported to improve vision and make glasses unnecessary in most cases.

Although Ha O Lin's school has examinations and gives grades, they are considered less important than behaving well and getting along with others. Ha O Lin's parents are proud that she volunteers to help handicapped children go to and from school. There is also a study hall at school where she helps slower learners in math, her best subject.

Afterschool activities are an important part of Ha O Lin's day. From 3:30 P.M. until 5:00 P.M. most days, she plays on the school grounds. When there are many children playing, she likes volleyball, badminton, and tug-of-war. When Ha O Lin is with just a few friends, she skips Chinese jump rope, which is played with a double rope. Sometimes two of her playmates stretch out a long piece of elastic, while others jump over it. They try to jump higher and higher without touching the elastic.

The whole neighborhood where Ha O Lin lives helps organize special afterschool activities. Retired workers are in charge of these activities, and they arrange discussions of current events and lead visits to theaters and museums. Today Ha O Lin changes into a gym suit that has trousers and a drawstring waist because she is doing *wushu* (Chinese fencing) with a special teacher. The teacher is also the grandfather of one of her good friends.

Every Friday afternoon Ha O Lin is lucky enough to visit the *Ching An*, Shanghai's "Children's Palace," where she studies music and practices her hobbies. It is on a magnificent hundred-year-old estate that was once the mansion of a British official.

After school, young people can play games, practice hobbies, or learn new skills at a Children's Palace.

The Ching An is a busy place. Two thousand children ages nine to sixteen from all over the city go there once or twice a week. It focuses on ballet, model-building, music, calligraphy, painting, electronics, and metalwork. The students are selected by their teachers and fellow students for the honor of attending.

While Ha O Lin is learning the Chinese harp, other children are involved in making models of planes and ships, trying out a sunflower dance that comes from Mongolia, and working in the machine shop. Still others are practicing acupuncture, a form of medical treatment, on each other. In this treatment long needles are inserted into different parts of a person's body. The children have been taught where the acupuncture points are located, so that they can stick the needles in the proper places.

The program at Ha O Lin's school as well as most of her afterschool time is planned. When she does have free time at home, she likes to play the game of Go (*weiqi*) on the sidewalk, chalking in the game board, and to read pocket-sized comic books.

Ha Wang Chu, Ha O Lin's brother, is very good at gymnastics. Twice a week he goes to a spare-time physical education center that is new in Shanghai. This center trains students in ping-pong, Western and Chinese gymnastics, volleyball, football, and track.

The children who attend it all have different abilities, and they are chosen from nearly two hundred schools.

As with the Children's Palace, the center is a place for serious fun. It supplies uniforms and sports clothing free of charge and lets students enjoy themselves while they develop their athletic abilities. In return, they are expected to teach the skills they learn to their classmates back at school.

Even very young students are given gymnastics lessons in Chinese schools. The best students may be chosen to attend a special physical education center, where they can develop their skills.

Right now Ha O Lin thinks that she would like to be a musician when she grows up. She imagines how she would accompany the singing part of the Chinese opera with her harp. Yet she knows that if she cannot reach her goal of becoming a musician, another job will be found for her. That is why she would also enjoy working in an herb garden.

But whatever Ha O Lin does later on, she knows that she must put her talents to good use. She has already learned that the purpose of education in China is to help everyone develop skills that will contribute to the common good. And so whenever she talks about the future, she always stresses that her most important goal is "serving the people."

9. China at Play

At one time, educated people in China did nothing physically active. In ancient China, officials did not even walk when they went outside their homes. Servants carried them from house to house in palanquins, little coaches mounted on stretchers instead of wheels. The idea behind this practice was that farmers and craftspeople worked with their hands, while educated people worked with their brains.

Mao Zedong completely changed this idea. He

taught that all people should use both their hands and their brains. That is why all students are expected to spend some time working in the fields and factories.

Almost everyone in China also follows or plays sports. A favorite pastime is to watch teams representing the nation or a commune play sports that are important in other countries. Basketball is the most popular team sport, followed by soccer and volleyball.

There are no private teams like the Pittsburgh Steelers or the Baltimore Orioles in China, though. And taking part in sports is considered better than watching them. In addition, fighting sports such as boxing are illegal, as is gambling.

"Friendship first, competition second" is Mao Zedong's teaching on sports. This principle goes beyond the Western idea of fair play because it puts good sportsmanship before winning.

Mao's favorite sport was swimming in one of China's many rivers. In the mid-1960s, there were many rumors that Mao had fallen seriously ill and was no longer able to govern. Some people even said that he was dead. But on a hot summer's day in 1966, seventy-three-year-old Mao completely surprised everyone by swimming nine miles (about fourteen kilometers) down the Yangzi River. This proof of his physical fitness made swimming more popular than ever with the Chinese.

Doing exercises is another way that people in China keep fit. From dawn until it is time to go to work, people of all ages gather in parks and along quiet streets to do *tai ji quan,* a series of 128 slow body movements. The idea of these movements is to keep your body in constant motion without losing your balance. A person doing them looks as if he or she is slowly wrestling against an invisible opponent.

Sometimes Westerners call tai ji quan a martial, or fighting, art, because it used to be an exercise for warriors. But since the Communist Revolution, millions of Chinese have done it to wake up their minds and bodies in the morning. For every American jogger, there are a hundred Chinese trying to perfect their skill in doing tai ji quan.

The rhythmic movements of this exercise demand great muscle control. But you also need to relax your mind and control your breathing to do them properly.

Although the tai ji quan exercises are often a group activity, they can be done by just two people. In this case, the action looks faster and more like shadow boxing. The pair doing the exercises may even use swords and spears. Yet though the two of them appear to be fighting, they never touch each other.

Most of tai ji quan's basic positions are named after animals and birds—eagle, bear, dog, dragon, monkey, horse, cat, leopard, lion, crane, dog, and snake. Another important position is called scissor-and-crossed legs. All of these graceful movements have even been worked into Chinese opera.

Factories as well as schools take breaks for exercises such as tai ji quan. The factories also have their own ping-pong and badminton competitions, and organize their own sports teams. A shoe factory team, for example, will compete against one from a printing plant.

In the winter, workers, university students, and high school pupils skate during their lunch hour. In the far regions of China, where people have no gymnasiums or stadiums, more traditional exercises and sports are popular. The Mongolians, for example, use their horses for games and competitions. And Tibetans enjoy a form of folk dancing that is as active and fast as any sport.

Chinese children learn and play sports in schools and youth centers. Many youngsters take gymnastics classes at school. Starting in grade school, they learn to do handsprings and flips, to swing on the high bar, and to vault. Doing these things well requires strength, a good sense of balance, and lots of hard work.

Students who are very good at gymnastics leave their regular schools and attend special ones that teach sports. Here they must practice long hours each day to perfect their skills. Boys work on floor exercises, the pommel horse, rings, the long horse vault, parallel bars, and the horizontal bar. Girls practice on the balance beam, the side horse vault, uneven floor bars, and floor exercises. The best students at these schools go on to be members of national teams that represent China in world competition.

Basketball and soccer, both new sports in China, are also becoming popular with children. Ping-pong is still one of their favorite sports, though. In Nanjing the Children's Palace has a large room filled with ping-pong tables, and they are in constant use when the center is open.

Adults play ping-pong as much as the children. In some parts of China, concrete ping-pong tables have been built so that people can play year-round.

In 1971 the Chinese government used ping-pong to establish relations with the United States. At that time there had been almost no contact between the two countries since 1949. But after the Chinese competed in the 1971 world table tennis championships in Japan, the U.S. team was invited to visit China for a series of matches. This invitation was a sign that the Chinese wanted to open talks with the United States. And the "ping-pong diplomacy" helped bring President Nixon to China in 1972.

Ping pong is one of China's most popular sports.

Chinese athletes are especially skilled in sports that require players to be quick, such as ping-pong, badminton, and volleyball. Yet they are beginning to try sports in which players must also be strong and durable. In 1980, for example, China had its first ice hockey tournament. This sport was not even known in the country until 1949.

Besides playing or watching sports, the Chinese enjoy a variety of leisure-time activities. One of them is strolling through the country's parks. China has some of the most famous parks in the world. Kublai Khan built a great park in Beijing in which he planted every kind of tree he could find. In Hangzhou another emperor built West Lake Park and stocked it with many varieties of goldfish. Under the emperors, only a few people could use these magnificent parks. Today they are open to everyone.

Many parks have cultural centers for the whole family. In Canton there is an open-air cultural center that is popular on hot summer evenings. It costs only a fraction of a yuan (the basic unit of money in China) to enter, and young people can play sports while older people have a game of chess. Sometimes schools put on concerts. Even kindergarten-age children perform hours of song and dance.

Indoors at the center people can play ping-pong or roller-skate. In one spot large groups gather to watch TV during the hours that the state channel has its broadcasts. In another place people learn chess by using pokers to move large-sized playing pieces across a gigantic chess board. The cultural center also has an exhibit hall for paintings, and a sports arena.

Card games are very popular in China. Once Chinese cards were long and narrow, but now they are shaped like Western cards. The card game the Chinese like most today is *pai-fen*, or "full mark." It is played until one person has scored one hundred points.

Board games such as chess and dominoes have been played in China for centuries. Chinese chess is something like Western chess. Basically, it is a contest between two armies. Each army is led by a general and his two officials, who direct the operations of their elephants, horsemen, infantry, cannon, and war chariots from a stronghold. These playing pieces are all very similar, being red on one side and black on the other. The object of the game is to destroy your opponent's general.

Chess is mainly a game for adults. Children prefer to play at simpler things, and their games vary with the season. One circle game involves passing a shuttlecock, a rounded playing piece having a flat end stuck with feathers, with the side of a player's heel. The object of the game is to pass the shuttlecock from person to person without it hitting the ground. Hopscotch is especially popular during the winter months, as is twirling tops on the frozen ground. Big children use whips that spin the tops at an extremely high speed for a very long time.

When the weather turns warm, kite flying becomes the favorite activity. Chinese kites come in all shapes and sizes, and often have fancy tails. The biggest kites are thirteen to sixteen feet (four to five meters) high. It takes several people to hold them by the tail once they're up.

The two main types of kites are soft wing and hard wing. The soft-wing kind can be folded in a box. People like to send them as gifts to relatives and friends who live far away. When these kites fly, their wings flap and make a beating noise in the wind. The hard-wing kite is made such that the body, head, and wings are joined into a single piece.

Kites have been flown in China since the ninth century. At first they were used for practical purposes, but in the tenth century people began to fly them for fun. Marco Polo once saw a wooden kite made of silk and bamboo that could lift a man into the sky. This type of kite was used to forecast the weather and to spy on enemy troops during battle.

Sometimes kites were flown just before the results of the examinations given to select government officials were announced. People who had taken the tests packed a picnic lunch and went into the hills to fly the kites. They believed that the higher a kite flew, the better they had done on the examination.

For hundreds of years the Chinese also delighted in having wandering entertainers visit their villages. These players performed with bears, dogs, monkeys, mice, and puppets. Acrobats, jugglers, stilt-walkers, and storytellers were also part of the show.

Today these entertainers have been organized into official touring groups, or troupes, of performers, and they follow a route decided on by the government. The best troupes are sent to places where people do not have many theaters, cultural centers, or sports stadiums, such as in Mongolia and Tibet. These people enjoy watching the tightrope walkers, trapeze artists, jugglers, and acrobats who visit them.

The performers are expert at diving through hoops, batting huge jugs back and forth from head to head, balancing on high stacks of chairs, and twirling

The Chinese government has organized skilled entertainers into official touring groups. These entertainers are performing a "Lion Dance" for a Beijing audience.

Dalton Delan

Not all performers have become part of a government troupe.
This street acrobat and his partner still put on their own shows.

rings, plates, or giant cards. Some of the acrobats are especially good at one skill or another, but everyone in the troupe tries to do as many things as possible.

When a group of entertainers arrives in a village on the plains of Mongolia, or in another part of China where ways are not yet modern, they are given a huge welcome. Often they perform outdoors, with the crowd sitting on carpets spread out on the ground.

Once the show begins, the audience fastens its eyes on the performers. No one moves or talks until an act is finished. After the entertainment ends, the whole troupe is invited to a village feast. Their performances are very important to people who have little contact with the outside world most of the year.

All of China's acrobats, entertainers, and full-time athletes share the idea that they are performing in order to inspire and please the nation. They believe that they are lucky to be able to do full-time what everybody likes to do part-time—develop their physical skills and stay fit. None of them thinks first about being a winner or a superstar. For in China it is more important to give happiness than to win success.

10. The Chinese in the United States

In chapter one, we saw the many kinds of visitors—travelers, merchants, diplomats, soldiers, and tourists—who came to China. Over the centuries, the flow was mostly one way. Travelers, traders, ambassadors, and armies came to China, but few Chinese ever left to go to other nations. The Chinese called their country the Middle Kingdom. They believed it was the center of the world and that other countries were not worth seeing.

In 1849 gold was discovered in California. At the same time, the southern province of Canton suffered a terrible drought. Many villages faced starvation, especially in a small county called Tai Shan.

In the port of Canton, the men of Tai Shan heard fantastic stories about the gold in California. Sailors and merchants told them it lay everywhere, and that it could be picked up right off the ground. Soon California became known as *gum shan*, "gold mountain."

Between 1849 and 1852, 25,000 men from Tai Shan and other parts of Canton Province sailed across the ocean to California. They were the first big group in China's history to leave their homeland.

At that time leaving China was against the law. The emperor was not powerful enough to keep Westerners out of his country, but he did try to keep the Chinese in. As a result, the first Chinese left secretly, taking only a few clothes and some money. Their wives and children stayed behind, hoping that the men would soon return home.

The Chinese who left their villages to find gold in California did not intend to stay in America. They only wanted to strike it rich and return to their homes as wealthy men. Only a few of them were successful. Most of them found little or no gold, and had to stay in America because they were in debt to a group known as the Six Companies.

The Six Companies were located in San Francisco. There was a company for each of the six areas in China like Tai Shan from which the Chinese had come. These companies lent the immigrants money to buy their passage to America and then helped them find jobs and housing when they arrived. Since the Chinese were poor villagers who spoke no English, they needed this kind of help.

Most of the immigrants borrowed quite a lot of money from the Six Companies, planning to pay it back when they found gold. Unfortunately, few of them found enough gold to pay back the money. The Six Companies would not let the Chinese return home until they had repaid their debt, however. As a result, these companies became very powerful. They were able to make the immigrants work for them. They also controlled the immigrants' social lives, running clubs where the men could relax and have fun.

Many of the Chinese who stayed in America became servants. They learned to cook, clean, garden, and do the laundry. Back in China, these jobs were considered to be women's work. But in America the men had no choice but to do them, since they had to earn a living. Almost every well-to-do California family had a Chinese servant.

During the days of the Gold Rush, the Chinese

often turned to laundry work. There were plenty of clothes for them to wash because the Americans who came West in search of gold didn't want to do laundry. They were rough and ready men who believed that washing clothes was women's work. Most of them hadn't brought their wives or children with them, though.

The Chinese took advantage of this situation by offering to do the men's laundry. They saw the work as a way for them to become independent, since all they needed to go into business for themselves was a bucket, a washboard, an iron, and an ironing board.

At first these laundrymen followed the gold prospectors. Later they went to the camps of the railroad builders. They spread out all over the country, and cities and large towns from San Francisco to New York soon had one or more Chinese laundries.

In time some of the men who had gone to work as cooks and servants were able to set up their own restaurants. They served food that was both delicious and inexpensive. Like the laundries, these Chinese restaurants soon spread to all parts of the country.

Today there are not many Chinese laundries because most American homes have automatic washers and dryers. But Chinese restaurants are more popular than ever. And even at non-Chinese restaurants, the chefs are often Chinese.

Many of the immigrants also became railroad builders. Before coming to America, few Chinese had ever seen a railroad. Yet soon after their arrival, many of them were hired to lay thousands of miles of train tracks.

The government was paying the railroad companies for every mile of track that was laid down. The more miles of track a company built, the richer it could become. But no company could grow wealthy unless it had fast, dependable workers, and at the time there was a shortage of these kinds of laborers. The Central Pacific Railroad turned to the Chinese immigrants, who had a reputation for being hard workers. It hired a team of fifty of them to see how well they would do at the job.

The Chinese proved to be excellent workers. They were not as strong as American laborers, but they worked more steadily. They didn't seem to slow down as day after long day and week after hard week passed by. In addition, they were efficient as a team because they really did help each other. And the Chinese workers did not have to be watched. They toiled just as hard when the boss wasn't around as when he was.

The Chinese railroad workers also became expert in handling dynamite. They were familiar with explosives because gunpowder had been invented and used in China for centuries. Still, dynamite was much more powerful and dangerous.

By 1869 the Chinese workers reached Promontory Point, Utah. There the Central Pacific joined its tracks with those of the Union Pacific to give America the first railroad that spanned the nation. To celebrate, an American railroad official drove in the last spike, a gold one. But it was the Chinese, though, who had conquered the mighty Sierra Nevada Mountains.

Once the Central Pacific Railroad was complete, the Chinese were out of jobs. Some of them went to build other railroads, while others worked on farms in the West. Still others found jobs in factories as far away as Massachusetts, and many became laborers on plantations in the South.

By this time 70,000 Chinese had come to the United States. Americans saw them as a strange group who, though hard workers and good cooks, seemed out of place. For Chinese men wore their hair in a long braid down the back. In addition, they dressed in baggy pants and loose shirts when they worked and in silk robes when they were at home. These Chinese clothes felt more comfortable to them than American ones.

In the 1870s the American economy went into a terrible slump. Wages declined and it was very hard to find work. Because the slump came so suddenly

Thousands of Chinese immigrants helped to build America's railroads. These workers are clearing snow for a route being constructed by the Northern Pacific Railroad in the Cascade Mountain range.

after a long period of high employment and good wages, most Americans could not understand what was happening. Confused and frightened, they looked for someone they could blame for their problems.

The Chinese, unfortunately, came in for much of the blame. People said that they had taken jobs away from American workers by accepting low wages. And they criticized the Chinese for not adopting American ways. People who could not speak English, who wore their hair in braids, and who dressed in silk robes did not belong in this country, they said.

Lawmakers soon began to take action against the Chinese as a result of this ill feeling. One law made it illegal for them to marry white people. Another taxed them at a higher level than other Americans because they had saved so much money. California even passed a Queue Law, which prevented Chinese men from wearing their hair in a long braid, or queue.

In 1882 the U.S. Congress passed the Chinese Exclusion Act, which denied citizenship to Chinese immigrants. It allowed only students, diplomats, and merchants to enter the United States, and they could not stay to become citizens. Ordinary Chinese were barred from the country altogether. This act marked the first time America closed its doors to immigrants. The law stayed in force until 1943.

The Chinese Exclusion Act also affected Chinese already in the United States. Many Chinese had come to America alone, planning to earn enough to bring their families over later. But after 1882 their families were forbidden to come. Later another law was passed which stated that if a Chinese American returned to China, he could never return to the United States.

Since the Chinese in America were not citizens and could not vote, they could do nothing to change these laws. Just how helpless they were is reflected in a popular expression that was coined at this time: "You don't stand a Chinaman's chance."

As Americans' dislike of the Chinese increased, many immigrants retreated into Chinatowns. These communities were named after the district in San Francisco occupied by the Six Companies. A city within a city, it was a place where everyone spoke Chinese, where shops sold Chinese goods, and where people could worship at Buddhist and Confucian temples. It even had its own hospital and system of law enforcement. Chinatown looked, smelled, and felt like a little bit of China itself. It was a place an immigrant could feel at home.

When the Chinese fanned out across America to work in factories, or on plantations and farms, Chinatowns sprang up in other parts of the country. The largest of them were in San Francisco and New York. They also developed in Boston, Chicago, Pittsburgh, and Los Angeles. In fact, more than twenty Chinatowns came into existence.

Yet even Chinatowns could not shelter the immigrants from hatred and violence. Time and again, angry crowds marched into these communities and destroyed property. And once more the Chinese could do nothing to stop them.

Unwelcome in white neighborhoods and disliked for living in their own communities, many Chinese men tried to escape their problems by gambling, drinking, and taking opium. But these things only made their situation worse. They also gave Chinatowns the reputation of being strange and evil places.

Had it not been for the Chinese Exclusion Act, life in America's Chinatowns might have been different. For its problems were mostly those of men without families. Yet the act barred Chinese men from marrying white women or from bringing their own wives and children from China.

When Congress voted to end the Chinese Exclusion Act in 1943, the wives and children of thousands of Chinese men were finally able to come to America. In fact, for the next ten years nine out of ten Chinese immigrants were women and children. During this time dislike of the Chinese lessened, and more and more families were able to move out of Chinatowns. As a result, these communities practically disappeared in small cities. In larger ones they became mainly places for shops, restaurants, and small factories.

Today San Francisco's Chinatown has many stores that sell herbs and traditional medicines. The walls of these shops are lined with hundreds of small drawers that contain remedies for illnesses. Each drawer is labeled with Chinese characters that tell what it holds—herbs, roots, minerals, or animal parts.

The customers who visit these stores sometimes know what they need. At other times they tell the shopkeeper what their problem is, and he decides what they should take. He may recommend powdered deer antler to reduce high blood pressure, Chinese rhubarb to calm an upset stomach, or ginseng root to improve blood flow. He may even sell someone bear's brain! It is believed to be a remedy for many ills.

Today many Chinese immigrants come from Taiwan and Hong Kong, and they often start their life in America in a Chinatown. They are called first generation immigrants. Their children, called the second generation, rarely stay in a Chinatown. They move to other neighborhoods and visit it on the weekend.

Second generation Chinese have common American first names. For example, the son of Kuang-fu Chu, whom we met in chapter one, is named Davy. Mr. Chu, his wife, and his son live in Brooklyn, New York. On the eve of the Chinese New Year, he and Davy usually go to Madison Square Garden and watch the New York Knickerbockers play basketball. The next day they have a traditional Chinese feast. Like many Chinese Americans, the Chu family is most Chinese at home.

Mr. Chu and his family are among the 500,000 Chinese Americans who now live in the United States. Many of these people are well educated and quite successful. Twenty-five percent of them go to college, a higher percentage than any other group of Americans. They are also entering the professions faster than non-Chinese. Many have become chemists, pharmacists, physicians, teachers, artists, engineers, architects, and computer programmers.

A number of Chinese Americans have achieved fame in art, science, or politics. The architect I. M. Pei designed Boston's Kennedy Memorial Library and a wing of the National Art Gallery in Washington. Tsung Dao Lee and Yang Chen Ning, professors of physics at Columbia University, won a Nobel Prize in 1957. Samuel Ting, another physicist, was a Nobel Prize winner in 1976.

Chinese Americans sometimes dress in traditional outfits to share their heritage with friends and neighbors.

Professor T.Y. Lin of Berkeley University started an engineering firm known for using concrete that is two times stronger than ordinary concrete. The steel it builds with is seven times stronger. Mr. Lin's company built the elevated roadway at San Francisco International Airport.

Hiram Fong's parents worked on a sugar plantation in Hawaii, and they could not read or write. He attended Harvard University and became the first senator to represent Hawaii after the state joined the union. March Eu Fong, another child of poor, hard-working parents, was raised in the back part of a hand laundry. She became both the first Asian American and the first woman to serve as California's secretary of state.

Don Kingman is a well-known painter, and James Wong Howe won Oscars for his camera work on two Hollywood films, *Hud* and *The Rose Tatoo*. Maxine Kong is a best-selling author who writes about Chinese immigrants to California.

Although the Chinese have adopted most American ways, they still want to preserve their own heritage. They have maintained thriving communities in the Chinatowns of New York, Boston, San Francisco, and Chicago. They go to Chinese shops, restaurants, and community events. Their families gather together to celebrate traditional Chinese holidays. And parents teach their children to respect old people, to prize education, and to be good workers.

The Chinese came to America in the hope of making a better life for themselves and their families. They stayed despite many disappointments and much harsh treatment. Through their hard work, cookery, and achievements in the arts and sciences, they have made America a better place to live for all its citizens.

Appendix A

List of Chinese Consulates in the United States and Canada

The People's Republic of China has embassies in both the United States and Canada, as well as consulates in several Canadian provinces. These places can provide you with fact sheets about Chinese life. They will also tell you how to obtain English-language books, magazines, and pamphlets that are put out by the China Publications Center in Beijing.

United States

Washington, D.C.
Embassy of the People's Republic of China
2300 Connecticut Avenue
Washington, D.C. 20008
Phone (202) 667-9000

Canada

Ottawa, Ontario
Embassy of the People's Republic of China
411-415 Saint Andrew Street
Ottawa, Ontario K1N 5H3
Phone (613) 234-2706

St. Johns, New Brunswick
Harold E. Kane, Honorary Consul
People's Republic of China
70 Germaine Street
St. Johns, New Brunswick E2L E27
Phone (506) 693-2681

Vancouver, British Columbia
Consulate General of the People's Republic of China
3338 Granville Street
Vancouver, British Columbia V6H 3K3
Phone (604) 736-6784

Appendix B

Resources for Teachers

Ambrose, Catherine. *Illustrated Map of China and Teachers Resource Sheet.* New York: Friendship Press, 1969.

Butts, Miriam, and Heard, Patricia. *The New American China Trade: "Foreign Devils to Canton."* Multi-Media Material, 342 Madison Avenue, New York, New York 10017.
> Kit of reproduced documents.

The Center for Teaching About China, 407 South Dearborn, Suite 945, Chicago, Illinois 60605.

China Books and Periodicals, 125 Fifth Avenue, New York, New York 10007.
> A supplier of China publications, including English language children's paperbacks, posters, records, and papercuts. Also distributes *China Pictorial,* a magazine with color photographs and short articles that is intended for students in the upper elementary grades and junior high school.

Chinese Cultural Activities, volumes I and II. New York: A.R.T.S., 32 Market Street, New York, New York 10002.

Echoes of China. Children's Museum, 300 Congress Street, Boston, Massachusetts 02210.

Whole kits or individual curricular units may be rented.

Information Center on Children's Cultures, 331 East Thirty-eighth Street, New York 10016.

Distributes "China in Children's Books," an up-to-date list of new titles, books on hard to locate topics of special interest, and books from small, specialized publishers.

Metropolitan Museum of Art. *A Chinese Village.* New York: Farrar, Straus & Giroux, 1980.

A construction kit.

Pellowski, Anne. *Chinese Folk Tales, Legends, Proverbs, and Rhymes.* CMS Records, 14 Warren Street, New York, New York 10007, 1970.

Disc or cassette recordings.

Project on Asian Studies in Education (PASE), 108 Lane Hall, University of Michigan, Ann Arbor, Michigan 48109.

Has resource list and lends audiovisual materials and books for one-month loan periods at little or no cost.

Sive, Mary Robinson. *China.* New York: Neal-Schuman, 1982.

A selection guide covering Chinese Americans as well as the People's Republic, with cross-media comparisons.

Appendix C

The Pinyin Writing System

As explained in chapter two, the Chinese writing system uses characters instead of an alphabet. At first these characters were like pictures of the things they stood for. Later they were changed into ideographs, which represent ideas rather than objects.

In the mid-1950s, Chinese schools began teaching their students *pinyin,* a system of writing Chinese in the Roman alphabet. Then in 1979 the Chinese government began using the Pinyin system in news reports and other communications that were sent to other nations. Today Pinyin is the officially approved system for spelling Chinese names and words used in English and other foreign languages.

The Pinyin system replaced all other ways of writing the Chinese language in the Roman alphabet. Among them was the Wade-Giles system, which was developed by two British diplomats, Thomas Wade and Herbert Giles, during the late 1800s and early 1900s. Many of the more familiar spellings of Chinese words and names are based on this system.

All of these spellings have been changed since the government adopted the Pinyin system. Peking is now written as Beijing, Yangtze River as Yangzi River, and Hangchou as Hangzhou. Similarly, Mao Tse-tung is now spelled Mao Zedong, and Chou En-lai as Zhou Enlai.

Government officials believe the Pinyin system best represents the way Chinese names and places are actually pronounced. It is not used in all English-language materials concerning China, but it seems to be gaining widespread acceptance.

Glossary

An Lu-shan (A.D. 703-757)—a general of Turkish descent who tried to found a dynasty and replace the Tang emperor in A.D. 755; he captured the imperial capital, but was murdered by a slave

cha—the Chinese word for tea, China's favorite drink

Chiang Kai-shek (1887-1975)—a military leader and president of the Republic of China; he and his followers set up a government on the island of Taiwan in 1949, after being driven from mainland China by Mao Zedong

Confucius (551-479 B.C.)—the founder of a philosophy that stressed high moral standards and attention to duty, manners, and ritual; his ideas have influenced the Chinese for thousands of years

Genghis Khan (1167-1227)—the most famous of the warrior-emperors of China; he began his conquests in northern China, took Beijing in 1215, and in the ten years that followed overran Asia, conquered Iran, and invaded Russia

gum shan—"gold mountain"; the name that people living in the Chinese province of Canton gave to California during the days of the Gold Rush

Han dynasty (202 B.C.-A.D. 220)—the period of Chinese history when the eastern half of China was united under the Han rulers, who based their government on the philosophy of Confucianism

Kublai Khan (1216-1294)—the grandson of Genghis Khan and founder of the Mongol dynasty that ruled China for a hundred years; under his rule, art and science flourished, and relations were established with many countries

laodong—an idea that is taught in Chinese schools; it means that people should always put their skills to productive use

Mandarin—the dialect of North China that was once spoken by Chinese public officials; today it is the form of the Chinese language taught in China's schools and in other countries

Mao Zedong (1893-1976)—the son of peasants, leader of the struggle that made China a Communist nation, and the chairman of the Chinese Communist Party from 1949 until his death

Mong Tian—the general who directed the building of the Great Wall; some 300,000 men, many of them prisoners, labored under Mong Tian's harsh command

nian hua—decorative New Year's pictures, a 1,000-year-old folk art in north and northeast China

pai-fen—a popular Chinese card game

Pinyin—a writing system that represents the Chinese language in the Roman alphabet; it is the system officially approved by the People's Republic of China for spelling Chinese names used in English and other foreign languages

qi-lin—an imaginary beast having a tiger's head, a man's face, long limbs, four hooves, and a snake between its teeth

Qin—the northwestern Chinese state that gained victory over rival states in the third century B.C.; under its rulers China became a unified empire for the first time

Qing Ming—"Pure Brightness"; a Chinese festival celebrated in early April; during it people visit the graves of their ancestors and go on picnics

Qins—a tribe of Tartar Turks who lived in Manchuria; in the twelfth century they invaded China and defeated the Song emperor, ruling the north of China for 150 years

Qin Shi Huang (246-210 B.C.)—the ruler of the Qin state who conquered and united China in 215 B.C.; he declared himself the first emperor

tai ji quan—a form of exercise that consists of 128 slow body movements

Tian An Men—"Gate of Heavenly Peace"; the square in Beijing where Mao Zedong proclaimed the formation of the People's Republic of China in 1949

weiqi—a Chinese children's sidewalk game

Wu Di—the most famous ruler of the Han dynasty (202 B.C.-A.D. 220); known as "The Martial Emperor," he ruled for fifty years and led wars against the peoples who roamed close to China's borders

wushu—Chinese fencing

Xandu—the gardens Kublai Khan planted at his palace in Beijing

Zhou Enlai (1898-1976)—premier of China who opposed the extremes of the Cultural Revolution and established diplomatic relations with the countries of the West and with Africa

Selected Bibliography

People's Republic of China

Boase, Wendy. *Early China.* New York: Watts, 1978.

Borja, Robert, and Borja, Corinne. *Making Chinese Papercuts.* Chicago: Albert Whitman, 1980.

Carter, Michael. *Crafts of China.* Garden City, New York: Doubleday, 1977.

Cesarani, Gian Paolo. *Marco Polo.* New York: Putnam's, 1982.

Cheng, Hou-Tien. *The Chinese New Year.* New York: Holt, 1976.

Christensen, Barbara. *Myths of the Orient.* Milwaukee: Raintree, 1977.

Kendall, Carol, and Yao-wen Li. *Sweet and Sour Tales from China.* New York: Seabury, 1979.

Kuo, Louise, and Yuan-Hsi. *Chinese Folk Tales.* Millbrae, California: Celestial Arts, 1976.

Lewis, Richard, ed. *The Luminous Landscape: Chinese Art and Poetry.* New York: Doubleday, 1981.

Mann, Shiah. *Chinese New Year.* New York: A.R.T.S., 1976.

Rau, Margaret. *The Giant Panda at Home.* New York: Random House, 1977.

————. *The People of New China.* New York: Messner, 1978.

Sadler, Catherine Edwards. *Two Chinese Families.* New York: Atheneum, 1981.

Shiu-ying, Fung. *Chinese Children's Games.* New York: A.R.T.S., 1974.

Tang, Yungmei. *China, Here We Come: Visiting the People's Republic of China.* New York: G.P. Putnam's, 1981.

Wolff, Diane. *Chinese Writing: An Introduction.* New York: Holt, Rinehart, & Winston, 1975.

Chinese in the United States

Bales, Carol Ann. *Chinatown Sunday: The Story of Lillian Der.* Chicago: Contemporary Books, 1973.

Perrin, Linda. *Coming to America: Immigrants from the Far East.* New York: Delacorte/Dell, 1981.

Pinkwater, Manus. *Wingman.* New York: Dell, 1975.

Sung, Betty Lee. *An Album of Chinese Americans.* New York: Watts, 1977.

Yep, Laurence. *Child of the Owl.* New York: Harper & Row, 1977.

———. *Dragonwings.* New York: Harper & Row, 1975.

———. *Sea Glass.* New York: Harper & Row, 1979.

Index

About the Authors

Chris and Janie Filstrup are well qualified to write about China for young people. Chris Filstrup is Chief of the Oriental Division at the New York Public Library. Janie Filstrup is a free-lance writer, who was formerly the Assistant Director, Information Center on Children's Cultures, U.S. Committee for UNICEF.

The Filstrups have written on the Middle East, Japan, child-rearing, families, and the arts. Their work has appeared in the *American Book World Geography*, *Children's Literature*, *Horn Book*, *New York Magazine*, and *Parents Magazine*. They are also the authors of *Beadazzled, The Story of Beads.*

Mr. and Mrs. Filstrup met while they were completing their master's degrees at Harvard University, Boston, Massachusetts. Later they lived in Iran for two years while teaching at the Tehran International School. Today they make their home in Bronxville, New York, with their children, Emma and Burton.